Development Planning for Primary Schools

by

Martin Skelton, Graham Reeves, and
David Playfoot

Published by The NFER-NELSON Publishing Company Ltd.,
Darville House, 2 Oxford Road East,
Windsor, Berkshire SL4 1DF, England.

First published 1991
© *1991, Martin Skelton, Graham Reeves and David Playfoot*

Printed by Billing & Sons Ltd, Worcester

ISBN 0 7005 1272 1
Code 8640 01 3

CONTENTS

Acknowledgements

Three groups of people have contributed much to the writing of this book and we would like to offer them our thanks.

First, the members of staff in our own schools who have taken part in and contributed to the process of identifying strengths and weaknesses, defining priorities and creating action. While the outcomes have often been positive, the journey has inevitably been difficult on occasions. Their willingness to take part has been both crucial and, hopefully, rewarding.

Second, the many teachers, headteachers, advisers and inspectors with whom we have worked in schools, and authorities throughout the country who have shared with us their experiences of development planning more openly than we might reasonably have expected. A special thanks is also due to those working in the schools which form our case studies.

Third, the teachers and headteachers of schools in the London Borough of Bromley, many of whom have been working towards effective school development planning for over four years now. For the first three years of that work much of the stimulus and drive was provided by David Beniston, Staff Inspector, and Gerald Grainge, Director of Education, in conjunction with a working party of headteachers and teachers. We are immensely grateful for all their support, insight and stimulation.

Preface

Nothing succeeds as planned.

These may seem strange words with which to begin a book
written with the specific intention of helping everyone who has
responsibility for the education of young people to create effective
plans for the development of their schools.
We have chosen these words because they emphasise that the
creation of a plan doesn't guarantee success. Things go wrong
along the way; situations change; the agenda shifts; we are asked
to respond to new initiatives – some important and worthwhile,
others less so; funding materialises and dematerialises, sometimes
responding to need, at other times responding to the prevailing
political climate.

In a time of increasing complexity, the usefulness of development
plans in helping schools define a workable, reasonable and
practical plan of action seems to us beyond doubt. The message
we hope to convey in this book is that the way in which the plan is
developed, the way in which it is implemented and the way in
which it stays relevant to both local and wider considerations are
as important as the existence of the plan itself – and all of these
have to be thought about and managed. This management of the
process of development planning is itself a complex task, and we
hope our book will help headteachers, teachers and governors
identify some of the issues and devise strategies appropriate to
their schools. School development planning is still in its infancy.
Our own ideas and approaches are being refined all the time as,
we are sure, are those of teachers, governors and heads involved
in their own schools. Our own experiences have taught us not to
believe that there is one true way and not to expect too much of
the development plan itself. We set it to sail on some very choppy
seas; without our constant attention and willingness to accept that
it can't make the journey on its own, it is almost certain to
founder.

All three of us have been both classroom teachers and
headteachers. Graham is a headteacher now; Martin and David are
partners in the educational INSET and consultancy group,
Fieldwork Ltd. We have all had experience of development
planning in our own schools; Fieldwork has also worked with a

number of local authorities and many individual schools in
helping to both begin the process of development planning and to
move it forward. Most importantly, we have all had personal
experience of setbacks as well as successes. The lessons learnt
through the setbacks have been vital and we have tried to share
many of them in this book. The progress gained through the
successes has been rewarding and has convinced us that, for now,
school development planning is the most important tool we can
use to create a clear direction from the many demands being
placed upon us.

It is important that schools begin to be pro-active again, but
professionally pro-active in a way which provides positive
outcomes for each school and gains respect in the wider
community education serves. School development planning
provides a framework within which such action can take place. It
seems essential to us that we take advantage of it as soon as
possible.

Introduction 1

Why Development Plans Are Important

It would be hard to find anyone in education who is prepared to tell you that things have got easier over the past few years – and no one would believe them anyway. The sheer weight of government legislation is proof enough of new and increasing demands being made upon schools but, in addition to the pressure for curriculum change and adaptation, schools are also coping with an increased accountability, the devolution of many management tasks, the introduction of new technology and the realisation that for some time to come education is going to be in the political and public spotlight.

We are in a period of immense change. Change has always been a feature of schools but the pace and complexity of the current changes is greater than at any time since the 1944 Education Act. Teachers, headteachers and governors are faced with the management of a complex range of activities. If the organisation of effective learning for a class of mixed-ability children isn't difficult enough, schools are also having to respond to, for example

- the implementation of the National Curriculum, both within the school and across different phases of education
- the local management of schools
- open enrolment and its implications
- evaluation and assessment
- teacher appraisal
- effective staff development

and much more. You will no doubt be able to add to the list, and even sub-divide each point into a series of related tasks and demands.

All of this would be a difficult enough task, but it is taking place against a background of heightened awareness of the problems of education from the general public, and a range of expectations from many sectors of society which are sometimes confused, often contradictory and occasionally just unrealistic.

We are currently being watched very closely, and, as a colleague on a course we were running said, "It's as though we are in the circus ring, with every move being watched by the audience – and the trouble is that some of the audience are booing even before we have begun our act!"

The question is, how do we cope with all of this? No one denies that to ask schools to successfully implement all the changes demanded of them simultaneously is a totally unrealistic demand – no one that is, except certain politicians for whom the political necessity of presenting an improved education service grows ever more pressing.

More realistic views than those held by some politicians can be found, however. In *Making Things Happen* John Harvey Jones talks of the minimum period of five years to effect any real lasting change – and even then we need to be going with the flow and not against it.

But five years may be too long for politicians, the public and the profession itself to wait. Talking in terms of five years can also provide a convenient excuse for actually doing very little; remember that the Russian economy was based on the idea of five-year master plans.

Schools have begun the 1990s with some difficulties. We have to respond to the demands being placed upon us. We have to respond to the public criticism as well as the occasional public praise. We have to find ways of restoring the relatively low morale among many of our colleagues. We have to find ways of becoming pro-active rather than reactive – in other words, to regain control over our progress and development. Where it has diminished, we have to face up to the responsibility to restore public confidence in the school system.

We won't do any of these things by rushing around desperately trying to cope with each new initiative and each new demand thrown at us. We won't do it by pretending that our schools are already superbly well organised where they are not. We won't do it by hiding our heads in the sands of everyday life in the hope that in a few years time the problems and demands will have gone away. They won't.

We have a chance of responding to the difficulties outlined above by understanding that planned progress towards a series of well-defined targets is the only reasonable strategy. School development planning is the framework within which such planned progress can take place.

What school development planning is about is the creation of realistic targets for the school which, over a period of time, address the school's strengths and weaknesses and create improvement in the education offered to the children. School development plans

- provide a direction to the school
- establish priorities
- provide a mechanism for reviewing progress
- enable a school to control – in a professional and understandable way – the rate and speed of its development
- allow for the appropriate involvement of others in the life of a school.

School development planning is as much about saying "No" as saying "Yes", but it is about saying "No" for professional, well-thought-out reasons rather than the understandable, if unfortunate, panic-button response of "We can't cope".

School development plans are also about enabling a school to present to its governors, its parents, the LEA and other interested parties some real evidence of the school's commitment to its development and some real evidence of its continuing progress towards the targets it has set. In this way school development planning is about regaining public confidence in schools.

Most importantly, school development planning is about giving teachers confidence that there is a direction, and that not everything has to be thought about, coped with and responded to at once. In giving this confidence, school development plans should enable teachers to concentrate on the most important aspect of their job – teaching children more effectively.

At a time when the pressures and demands on schools are so great we have to accept that responding to them all at the same time is impossible. We need a strategy and a direction and the clarity to put that strategy into practice.

The process of school development planning is not easy and we have written this book as one contribution towards helping schools overcome and deal with some of the hurdles. Our experience is that school development planning represents the best chance schools have of regaining and maintaining some stability.

The idea of school development plans is not new and a number of schools have planned their progress for some time now without, perhaps, ever calling the process school development planning. Over the past twenty years there have been two distinct drives behind the call for schools to plan their development more effectively. The first is to do with accountability.

On the one hand, this demand for accountability grew out of external pressures on schools to improve. During the 1970s schools increasingly came under public scrutiny. Disputes such as that surrounding the William Tyndale Primary School in London – however isolated and however inappropriately reported – began to fuel public speculation that all was not right with the education children were receiving. That no three people could agree on what was right is not the point; concern about schooling began to be widely expressed wherever a discussion took place.

This concern was picked up by governments who brought education to the forefront of the political agenda, not least by James Callaghan in his famous Ruskin College speech in which he ensured that the "secret garden" inhabited by teachers and other educationalists should be thrown open to all.

Such a view might have seemed a knee-jerk response to public disquiet but other arguments made a similar point from a different perspective. Arguments about the democratisation of schools made it clear that schools exist to educate children on behalf of parents and the community and not in spite of it, and that, this being the case, schools should be prepared to make clear to the community what they were doing.

The publication of HMI reports added fuel to the fire. These reports, while stressing the strengths of many schools, also exposed some of the weaknesses and challenged schools to deal with those weaknesses as soon as possible. In 1979, for example, the DES published *Aspects of Secondary Education* in which it said

"Within individual schools there is much stocktaking which many staffs could do for themselves in evaluating their own policies and practices ... in identifying priorities for their own future development and in deciding where a start can be made, according to the school's circumstances and present stage of growth".

This description of what we now know as school development plans
went largely unheeded and it is interesting to speculate on what might
have happened during the 1980s if most schools had picked up on
that recommendation when it was first made.

So the demands for accountability grew stronger and the need for
schools to identify a way of responding to those demands grew too.
School development planning, as described by the DES above, was
seen as one of the ways forward.

At the same time, the general level of demands on schools increased,
too. Perhaps because we weren't seen to be putting our house in order
quickly enough, perhaps because the debate about what sort of house
and what sort of order continued to rage or perhaps because the
chance of scoring some political capital was spotted the kinds of
demands listed in the previous section increased. The 1988 Act
represented the formal definition of many of those new demands
which have, to a large degree, been accepted across the political
spectrum. They are unlikely to change much whatever the
complexion of government throughout the 1990s.

However valuable each of the new demands might be it has quickly
become apparent that schools will have difficulty responding to them
all. To avoid the catastrophe of everything being attempted and
nothing being achieved the need for priorities within the context of
the "schools, circumstances and present stage of growth" has been re-
established. It is increasingly understood that without some form of
effective planning schools just haven't a chance of improving their
practice across the many fronts demanded.

The 1990 publication by the DES of the booklet *Planning for School
Development* – the first of a series – provided evidence of official
blessing for this process of prioritising and strategic planning – a
blessing which we believe schools would do well to take as seriously
as possible.

Three factors, then, have stimulated interest in school development
planning over recent years:

- a need to respond to arguments about accountability from those who
  perceive evidence that schools aren't as good as they ought to be
- a need to respond to arguments about accountability from a
  democratic movement which stresses the rights of parents and
  others to know what schools are doing

- a need to find a way through the complex demands schools have to face at the moment and will continue to face for the rest of the decade and beyond.

We believe it is a mistake to regard school development planning as just a current fad which will probably fade away. Schools do have many strengths at the present, but we exist in a public context which makes demands on us and to which we have to respond. School development plans should be here to stay.

The DES booklet *Planning for School Development* draws an important distinction between school development planning as a product and as a process. We think it is important that this distinction is made as clear as possible.

The product

School development planning produces a product – a school development plan. This plan needs to contain, at the very least

- the targets the school is hoping to achieve
- the time scale over which those targets are going to be tackled
- the particular responsibilities of different members of staff which will contribute towards achieving those targets
- the cost of achieving the targets and other resources needed.

In addition, a number of schools with whom we have worked have also included in their plans a résumé of the reasons why certain targets have been chosen (in practice this turns out to be a description of the review of the school) plus a description of how the relative success of the targets is to be evaluated.

This shouldn't be a lengthy document – indeed, the shortest and most easily accessible plan which contains all of the necessary information is, in our view, the best plan. You might need a slightly different and more comprehensive version of the plan for the use of the school staff than you would need to present to the governors and others, but the principle of shortest equals best still remains.

Many schools beginning development plans understandably need to have an image of what the document will look like in order to get started; the completion and publication of the plan is of great importance to them. We think the format of the plan is up to individual schools, although you will find one or two examples of sample formats on pages 110 to 116 of this book. Please treat them as guides. The plan you end up with has to be understood and used by the people working in and connected with your school.

The process

Having a completed school development plan isn't enough. In the end, what matters is whether the targets contained in the plan are achieved, and whether those targets were the right ones to enable the school to move forward as sensibly as possible.

Whether these two things happen depends very much on the way in which the plan was devised and the way in which it is going to be implemented – in other words, on the process of development planning. It is our experience that a number of schools fail to achieve as much success as possible because they have placed too much emphasis on the creation of the formal, written plan and not enough on the planning processes which surround it.

In some cases, for example, headteachers have formulated the plan on their own, only to find that the targets it contains are not agreed by everyone. At other times, the initial discussion of the strengths and weaknesses of the school has been inadequately or insensitively carried out causing targets to be defined which don't address the most important needs of the school, that cause upset and antagonism among the very staff for whom it should be a support.

Again, even when the formal plan has been devised as a result of a sensitive and careful analysis of the school's strengths and weaknesses, the process of beginning to work towards the targets can sometimes be inadequately thought through. We have all suffered from

- too many targets to be achieved in too little time
- no room for the inevitable crises which are a natural feature of school life
- resources not available
- no staff development allowed for colleagues having to face new challenges
- the abandonment of the plan's targets at the first hint of trouble
- the lack of anyone committed enough to provide support and stimulus to staff when the going gets tough.

Scenarios such as these can all contribute towards the process of development planning failing or achieving less success than it deserves. We believe that school development planning should be about maximising success and reducing failure. To achieve this success, the formal declaration of the plan is important; everyone needs to know where they are going and who is responsible.

But this formal declaration is not enough and cannot lead to success on its own. The processes of reaching the formal plan and the processes of implementing the action required to achieve its targets are also crucial. *Planning for School Development* suggests that schools go through three stages

- the need for and creation of a plan
- an understanding that the processes involved in creating and implementing the plan are important
- an understanding that the effective management of those processes is the real key to success.

Our experience of working with a number of schools supports that view. If you are beginning development planning for the first time or are in the process of reviewing the successes and failures you have achieved until now, it is vital that you spend as much time looking at the processes you went through to achieve and implement your plan as it is to look at the plan itself. On the following pages we present a model and description of the planning process.

Throughout this book we are indebted to the work of many headteachers, teachers and inspectors with whom we have worked throughout the country but particularly in the London Borough of Bromley. This model, in particular, owes much to their work.

The audit stage

The audit stage is concerned with identifying the strengths and weaknesses of the school as clearly as possible. It depends on an understanding that schools have strengths and weaknesses and that declaring them is not a weakness but a strength. Clearly it is a delicate stage and one in which the progress of the school can be set back for some time if the process is badly managed and executed.

Auditing involves
- developing a range of strategies which help to reveal the school as it is
- creating a climate which allows those strategies to be used positively
- considering the strengths and weaknesses against the ideal direction of the school
- accepting the inevitable and proper influence of the policies of the LEA and central government, recent school reviews and the views of others connected with the school.

Development involves

- responding to the weaknesses identified in the audit
- defining priorities
- agreeing time scales
- defining responsibilities
- working within the constraints imposed by finance and other resource implications
- accepting that realism is, at this stage, more important than idealism
- publishing the agreed plan as a formal statement.

Evaluation involves

- understanding that nothing succeeds as planned
- using appropriate methods to check how far the targets have been reached
- trying to identify the reasons for successes and failures – in other words, evaluating the process as well as the targets
- reporting the outcomes to various groups including the governors
- feeding the evaluation back into the next development stage.

Central to these is implementation. At each stage, the way a staff implements the audit, development and evaluation stages will be crucial. What is most important about development planning is the action it stimulates and the progress that is made, not the paperwork it produces. A concern for effective implementation involves thinking about

- sustaining commitment
- overcoming problems
- defining appropriate structures
- fostering appropriate involvement.

The relationship between the stages
Although we have described each of these stages separately we hope it is clear to you that this is only for the convenience of establishing and describing a model. In practice, the stages are inter-related. For example, in an ideal world each school would have a clear vision of where it is going against which its strengths and weaknesses could be evaluated. In practice this often isn't the case. A number of schools we have worked with have told us how the audit stage enabled them to begin to define more clearly what it was that mattered to them.

Similarly, although the evaluation stage is usually seen as the last stage of models such as this, the importance of evaluating the processes of school development planning as well as the outcomes means that some evaluation will be taking place all of the time. A model that represented the actuality of development planning would not be very accessible. So, interpret this model in the light of a series of inevitable inter-relationships between the various stages.

Where to begin

For some schools, the complexity of this relationship between the stages has created a feeling that they might as well start school development planning anywhere within the model. In our view this would be a mistake. Without a clear and agreed definition of the strengths and weaknesses of the school it is almost impossible to devise effective targets; without defining effective targets it is difficult to identify effective evaluation strategies.

In practice, we suggest that the process looks something like this:

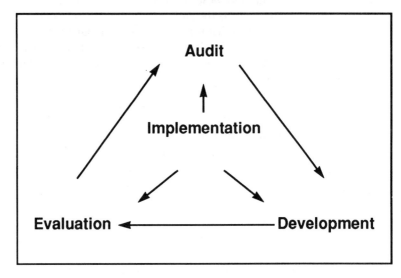

An initial audit is conducted, followed by the development stage, followed by the evaluation which then feeds back into the second development stage, a second evaluation and then a third development stage and so on. As staff and situations change every two or three years, it is a good idea to recreate the initial audit at those times, allowing a fresh look at what are perceived to be the school's strengths and weaknesses. At the same time, of course, the process needs to be monitored.

If the process of school development planning is about auditing, developing and evaluating then it is important to have a clear idea what is being audited, in what areas development should take place and what is being evaluated.

Schools are complex places. It is important that we should have a way of knowing that the school development planning process and the formal plan itself have not missed important areas of a school's life and work. The London Borough of Bromley have identified six Key Areas which they recommend form the focus of development plan thinking. We have found these areas to be useful both in our own work and in that of many other headteachers, teachers and governors.

1 The developing curriculum

Debates have raged endlessly about the exact meaning of the word 'curriculum', some of them more fruitful (for example, the distinction between the formal curriculum and the hidden curriculum) than others.

When we talk about the 'developing curriculum' in this context we are talking about the formal curriculum – the teaching that is planned by the school and its teachers to enable the children to learn.

Inevitably, at the moment, much of the work a school does in this area will be connected with the implementation of the National Curriculum. However, the National Curriculum doesn't represent all the teaching that a school plans.

The developing curriculum refers to the whole curriculum and will relate to the production of school policies, the implementation of those policies throughout the school and their review.

2 The staff

The school staff is probably its most valuable resource, and so quality is important. The most wonderfully written school policies are useless if they cannot be implemented by teachers in classrooms and it is a pointless exercise to begin producing such policies if we are not also prepared to take on board the responsibility of helping staff develop abilities, attitudes and competencies which enable them to cope more effectively.

The debate about whether staff development is an active or a facilitating role will continue for some time, although we believe that it is better to think of helping to create the conditions within which we can all develop than it is to think of the overt 'development' of colleagues (see also Section 4.2).

'The staff' as a key area reminds us of the fundamental importance of the whole staff to the school; to ignore the implications of that for professional and personal development is self-defeating.

3 The school constituency

It is nearly four years since a working party in Bromley defined 'the school constituency' as one of the key areas; no one really liked the title then and, even if we are all used to it by now, it's still not quite right. Any better ideas will be gratefully received!

'The school constituency' refers to the fact that schools are not insular places – they exist within and have responsibilities to a much broader group of people, organisations and formally constituted bodies. It refers to all of those identifiable individuals and agencies likely to influence or be interested in the effectiveness of children's learning – parents, other members of the local community, the governing body, the LEA and central government. Recent moves towards open enrolment have focused the attention of many schools towards the constituency which they serve and to which they are, in part, responsible. Examining the relationships between a school and its constituency involves identifying means of effective communication, consultation and participation.

4 Buildings and sites

No one doubts the importance of buildings and sites in contributing to the effectiveness of the education children receive. Although we have seen some quite tremendous education provided in appalling conditions and some pretty ineffective education provided in stupendous surroundings, there is a need to look at how the buildings and site enhance or reduce the education children are receiving and what can be done about it.

Equally, as a part of financial management, many schools are also looking at how effectively their buildings and sites are being used as a community resource or as a generator of income for the school.

5 Organisational systems

Many of us have worked in schools where the systems seem to take priority over the work. It wasn't too long ago, for example, that one of us worked in a school where the art stockroom was only open on Tuesday lunchtime, and only then if what you needed was written down in a specially provided little book.

Such experiences can heighten our understanding of just how important effective organisational systems can be to the smooth running of any organisation. Because schools are so complex, because they deal with so many different issues and because they deal with young people of different ages and experiences, effective and realistic organisational systems – from fire drill through financial budgeting through to inter-staff and departmental communication – can have an enormous impact on the relative success or failure of a whole range of actions.

Choosing 'organisational systems' as a key area reminds us of that importance.

6 The climate

Even though we all have an idea of what it means, 'the climate' is the hardest of the key areas to define. It is about the inter-relation of those factors which create and affect the atmosphere within a school and the image it promotes. The climate of a school affects the way in which work proceeds in the other key areas, but it is also affected by that work. Changes in climate cannot occur independently of that work – they are reflected through it.

'The Climate' is important because it is often the spark or extinguisher of activities. It is difficult to get hold of and can be threatening to consider, particularly when the climate of a school isn't perceived as good. But the whole development planning process needs an appropriate climate if schools are going to take full advantage of all that it can offer; for this reason it needs to be considered seriously.

Using the six key areas

There is nothing sacrosanct about the key areas we have outlined above. You may want to substitute different headings or even different categories. What is important is that you have some way of ensuring that all of the important aspects of your schools are being considered within the planning process and are subsequently reflected in your published plan.

Many headteachers and teachers with whom we have worked have found the key areas useful in focusing their own thinking, staff discussions and the format of the development plan they eventually adopt.

It is a good idea to subject each of the key areas to the audit – development – evaluation process. It doesn't mean that all of them will necessarily appear in your final development plan, but having given them each careful consideration you will be in a better position to support whatever decisions you finally reach about your targets.

Equally, in considering each of the key areas in turn you will be able to identify which aspects of your school are the real sticking points to progress. A teacher in one school told us:

"Like everyone else, we had committed a lot of time to the implementation of the National Curriculum but we didn't seem to have made the progress we should have, given how much time we had spent on it all. I don't mean that we should have cracked the whole thing and had it running smoothly – just that we should have been in a better position than we were.

It was about this time that we began the school development plan. At first, there were a number of us who were really cynical about the whole thing – you know, just more work on top of the work we already had. But our head was as worried by our lack of progress as we were and took the development planning meetings quite slowly and carefully.

We went through everything and lots of things were raised. Among the most important though were the fact that when we looked at 'organisational systems' we discovered that everyone was really fed up with inefficient meetings and with the fact that the same information never seemed to reach everyone. When we looked at 'climate' we found – not surprisingly – that because everyone was so fed up with our organisation they didn't really believe we'd make any progress at all and so didn't work as hard as they might have done.

This teacher's experience is not uncommon. By concentrating only on the National Curriculum – however sensible that might seem in the short term – it is quite possible for schools to miss some of the crucial factors which cause their National Curriculum planning to be less effective than it might be.

The six key areas are obviously inter-related. You may choose to begin by looking at 'the developing curriculum' first and considering the effects of this on the other five areas. You can then look at other aspects of those five areas subsequently. Over the next few pages, we will be looking at how the original audit can be carried out. It is worth bearing in mind that without the right climate, reasonable organisational systems and effective relationships with most of the school constituency, much of the work on the curriculum, buildings and sites or staff support and development will be wasted.

It isn't for us to tell you which of the key areas you concentrate on first when you begin development planning. The key areas on which you concentrate when you begin development plans depend upon your school. But we recommend that you use them to remind you of the breadth of your school.

2 Starting the Development Planning Process

Section 1.3 of this book briefly outlines and discusses the development planning process. Crucial to that discussion is the need to manage the process, to be constantly evaluating how the process is going, and be aware of whether the way in which the process is taking place is proving a help or a hindrance.

You'll remember that the DES document *Development Planning in Schools* suggested that for many schools the realisation that the process needed managing occurred only after they had discovered that a development plan wasn't enough in itself, and that simply to be conscious of the processes involved didn't ensure success either.

One of our reasons for writing this book has been to use our collective experience and that of the many schools with whom we have worked to try and encourage headteachers and teachers to increase the extent to which they understand that the process needs to be managed and to provide some hints on how that might best be done.

Nowhere is this more necessary than at the very beginning of development planning. Some schools have begun this in a very grudging sort of way, sidling up to it without the expectation that much will come of it. In some authorities they have been wise to take this approach; we heard, for example of one authority which had asked its schools (or rather, its headteachers) to write a development plan and submit it to the Director of Education within eight weeks of the initial request.

One of us can remember sitting in the staffroom of one school in that authority as the head explained to an in-the-dark staff that the development plan had been sent in over three months ago and that there was nothing to worry about.

On the other hand, some schools find themselves at the mercy of a headteacher or colleague who has seen the light and has become a school development plan convert. Full of messianic fervour, this person flogs everyone through the various stages so quickly that no one has a chance of airing any real views or finding out what is happening. This can be a particular problem when a new headteacher takes over a school and is determined to get things moving.

"I'd been at my new school for about three months. It's my first headship. My previous school had been involved in school development planning and I was quite impressed by what we had done. I gave myself what I thought was a reasonable amount of time to settle in and then set to.

I asked the staff for their views about the school, about our strengths and about our weaknesses – and I received them by the bucketful. Slightly overwhelmed, I began to sort them out and we started to look for priorities which we made pretty easily.

To cut a long story short, it was about a term later that I realised that we weren't really working towards our priorities at all. I began to try and find out why. My deputy told me in no uncertain terms one evening after school. All of the staff had responded only because I had asked them to – they had no commitment to or real knowledge of what they were doing.

The upshot of all this was that we had to have a sort of break from it all and start again the following term. Because I was so hasty and misread the situation we lost almost a year. It was crazy."

Preparing the ground – the importance of backstage work

When we go to the theatre, to the cinema or to a concert what we see is only the end product of an enormous amount of work we can't see. The rehearsals, the crises of confidence, the reassurance, the creation of the right ambience, the development of a common direction – all of these are important to the success or failure of what we will eventually see on the stage, and all of them take time.

The same process is vital in school development planning. The authority which demanded school development plans in eight weeks hadn't appreciated how much time the process can take to get off the ground. The headteacher who thrust development planning at her staff at the first available opportunity had simply assumed that her new group of colleagues were at the same point and shared the same views as the colleagues in her previous school. Both were wrong and both led to ineffective – or impotent – development plans being introduced.

A number of teachers spoke to us about the introduction of development planning into their schools.

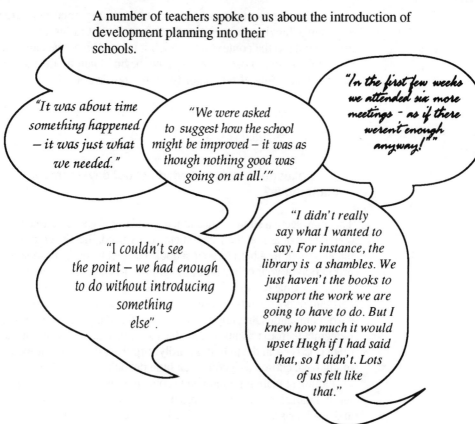

"It was about time something happened – it was just what we needed."

"We were asked to suggest how the school might be improved – it was as though nothing good was going on at all.'"

"In the first few weeks we attended six more meetings – as if there weren't enough anyway!'"

"I couldn't see the point – we had enough to do without introducing something else".

"I didn't really say what I wanted to say. For instance, the library is a shambles. We just haven't the books to support the work we are going to have to do. But I knew how much it would upset Hugh if I had said that, so I didn't. Lots of us felt like that."

Some of the responses were very positive; others were less so.

We haven't chosen these comments to prove a particular point. But their flavour is more common than many people realise. School development planning can be a threat, as many changes are a threat. It can call into question or reveal interpersonal difficulties between colleagues. It can appear to be more work rather than a strategy for working more efficiently. It can appear to be just another way in which headteachers try to get their own way.

All of these views are understandable. When we are beginning school development planning we are doing so in a context which can both help and hinder its progress. Our ability to understand that context and respond to it and our ability to create the conditions within which development planning has a chance to develop positively is crucial to its success.

School development planning is about identifying important targets and then achieving them – it is about success, not failure. If we misunderstand the context into which it is introduced we can sow the seeds of failure almost before we have begun. Gaining the support and understanding of the majority of the staff is crucial.

We have identified four important questions you might want to think about.

1 Are colleagues aware of what school development planning is?

This may seem a strange question, particularly if you are already convinced, or are on the way to being convinced, that development planning will be a help to your school. The fact is that a reasonable proportion of your colleagues might not be as clear. There are perfectly understandable reasons for this. Bombarded as they are by new curriculum documents, information about assessment and testing, curriculum audits, the implications of LMS and a wide range of value judgements from parents, the media and, it seems, almost anyone at a dinner party or in the pub, it is hardly surprising that some of them might have chosen to ignore what little publicity about school development planning might have come their way. We also need to remind ourselves that these same people are also having to plan, prepare and teach classes of up to 34 mixed-ability children at the same time!

Time needs to be spent helping colleagues understand that

- it is a way of prioritising what the school will do over a given period of time
- it is a way of helping to establish exactly what their particular responsibilities will be in school
- it is a way of involving governors and gaining their support for a carefully worked out programme of activities
- it is a way of using professional discussion as a means of saying 'No' to various initiatives as well as 'Yes'.

2 Are colleagues aware of what the development planning process involves?

There is no doubt that an effective development plan reduces the pressure on teachers and schools and enables a school to be more positive and more self-directed. But it would be stupid to pretend that there isn't a price to pay for that at the beginning and school development planning creates its own initial workload. Colleagues will need to be aware that

- it will require a number of meetings which may be in addition to those already being held (however, it is our view that if you want success you should, wherever possible, clear the decks of as many other meetings, INSET and school activities as possible)
- it will require joint decisions by the staff and a commitment to the decisions which have been reached
- it will often require job descriptions to be revised as a result of the priorities agreed during the process
- it will mean that it won't be possible for everyone's personal priorities for the school to be acted upon at once
- it will mean the publication of the agreed priorities, if only initially to the governors
- it might mean that the school could be reviewed on its success and failure at achieving the priorities set within the plan.

3 Are the relationships between colleagues strong enough to withstand the pressures ?

It is very easy to divorce the theory of development planning from the reality. In doing so we tend to forget that the process and its outcomes are taking place within the context of busy and sometimes difficult schools. The relationships between colleagues are an important factor in the relative success and failure of development planning. The process requires an openness and an honesty which some staff groups find difficult to achieve. It requires an atmosphere which is relaxed enough to allow open discussion and an inter-group confidence in which everyone is already aware that the work they do in the school is genuinely valued.

In many schools in which we have worked, the process has helped to foster good relationships; in others, unfortunately, it has foundered because of bad ones. There is no easy answer. What is certain is that relationships will never be perfect. What is important is that you don't begin the process of development planning without considering its effect on those relationships, or the effect those relationships will have upon it.

4 Is there a professional atmosphere in the school?

In their book *Appraisal and Professional Development in Schools*
Day et al said that "… schools seem to find their success depends
very much on a situation where the climate of a school … encourages
and accustoms staff to look critically at their own practice …"

That refers to the introduction of appraisal, but it might equally refer
to the introduction of development planning. Good relations between
colleagues are important, but to be really effective they have to be
maintained in a professional as well as a personal context.

Many of us have worked in staffrooms where the relationships are fine
as long as the discussion is kept to films we have seen, the weekend
ahead, newspaper headlines, and so on. These are important, but such
relationships are unlikely to really benefit the school unless they also
flourish in a professional context. You might like to consider the
following questions about your school, for example.

- Is there a shared understanding that few decisions about education
  are clear-cut and definitive?
- Is there an acceptance of professional discussion of the issues?
- How do staff – including yourself – respond to new issues and
  demands? Is the response a personal, knee-jerk one or is it more
  carefully and professionally considered?
- Are staff more or less aware of the issues surrounding their areas
  of responsibility and classroom teaching?

These might seem like reasons or excuses not to begin development
planning at all. We don't mean it to seem so. What we hope you will
avoid is rushing into the process without considering how much
back-stage work is required, without considering the context within
which development planning will begin.

The context will never be 'right' and the moment is never perfect.
However, maximum success depends on the best possible conditions. As
Hargreaves *et al* say in *The Management of Development Planning*

"In some schools, where the conditions to support innovation
already exist, development planning will be easily introduced and will
enhance the school's capacity to manage change. In schools where
these conditions do not exist, the chances of succeeding with
development are lower since the conditions themselves need to be
changed as an inherent part of the process of development planning."

What is it?

The audit is the first stage of the development planning process. It is a stocktake, an attempt to describe your school now. It requires an acceptance that the school has both strengths and weaknesses and a willingness to reveal them.

The audit stage has its own dangers. First, there is the chance that it is used only as an opportunity for self-congratulation; that the process identifies what staff believe to be good but ignores the weaknesses. On the other hand, there is the danger that masochistic organisations will use it to define how dreadfully they are doing, to set up recriminations and to ignore some of their successes.

The audit stage requires a cool appraisal of the situation. In identifying areas as either 'strengths' or 'weaknesses' you will need to ensure that the judgements of those involved are supported by some evidence. The audit stage cannot afford to take anything for granted – that is why it is important that a professional atmosphere should exist within the school. It is very easy to go through the audit stage superficially, but it is also very dangerous.

Why is it important?

The audit stage is important because from it will come

- the priorities which will be defined in the 'development' stage
- the staff responsibilities needed to achieve those priorities,
- a staff development programme
- a degree of financial investment
- and a not inconsiderable amount of work.

Eventually there will also come the evaluation of those priorities. This evaluation is important both for the internal and external confidence of the school. Externally, it is obviously important that the school should be seen to be well-organised and making progress, but the internal evaluation of the development plan and its process by the staff is also vital to the way in which the school develops.

It is right that development planning should result in success. For us this means that staff and others should be able to clearly identify what has happened and should be able to realise that the school has improved as a result of the efforts made. This is only really possible if the audit stage is effective. If the priorities targeted by the development plan respond to the real weaknesses of the school and the work resulting from those priorities improve the quality of what goes on, then the school is likely to be a better place. But so much depends on revealing – in a confident and supportive manner – exactly what those weaknesses are.

The audit stage of development planning requires very careful and sensitive handling. Without it, the whole process could be misrouted before it has begun.

Is it always necessary to start with the audit stage?

In our view, it is difficult to see how development planning can start anywhere else. We have worked with a few schools which seem to have begun at the development stage by committing themselves to priorities and working towards them almost immediately. Sometimes this might be appropriate. For example, we can think of one school which seemed to have made no attempt to sort out any form of coherent policy for teaching English, mathematics and science to children working through Key Stage 1 of the National Curriculum. Quite rightly, the new headteacher of that school made it a priority; within two months of her arrival such a policy existed.

Nevertheless, some auditing had still taken place. The headteacher, along with other members of staff, had conducted a quick review of the school and had identified an obvious and very pressing need. In many ways this represented a form of crisis management, but what happens in crisis management is that the initial audit simply takes place very quickly, usually because a particular need is very clearly identifiable.

So some form of initial audit takes place even in crisis management; it is the speed of the audit which changes, not its use.

What are the links between audit and evaluation?

The audit stage and the evaluation stages can appear to be very similar, but while they serve similar functions there are important differences.

The audit stage serves to provide an accurate description of the school as it is now. In identifying strengths and weaknesses, the reality is that staff and others are often doing so against an implicit understanding of what represents a 'good' school.

In the evaluation stage, what is being evaluated and assessed is much more explicit since it is defined by the priorities the staff have chosen as the focus of their development plan. Our experiences in schools have suggested to us that evaluation is inevitably a much more focused activity than the initial audit.

Because of this focus, the methods used in the evaluation stage can be more sophisticated than those used in the audit stage. We will be looking at ways of both auditing and evaluating in later sections of this book.

Evaluation is a permanent part of the development planning process; whenever priorities exist and are being worked towards there needs to be a regular evaluation of how well the school is doing. The audit, however, seems to be most effective when carried out at less regular intervals. It is vital as a first stage to the whole procedure but it is unlikely that all of the weaknesses it reveals can be included in the initial development plan; it is equally unlikely that all the priorities and targets of that first development plan will be achieved with equal success.

The targets and priorities of the second development plan, therefore, are likely to consist of a reworking of some of the initial targets plus some of the originally identified weaknesses which were considered important but which could not be included in that first plan.

A second audit is likely to be most beneficial every two or three years when a number of targets have been agreed, worked towards and met. It is at this point that you are likely to find another more general description of where the school is – given the demands being made upon it – more useful.

There is one obvious answer to this question – the headteacher and the staff of the school. They are the ones responsible for the work which takes place and they are the ones who will have to carry out much of the work which leads to the achievement of the priorities contained in the plan.

But our work with schools has revealed considerable discussion about who else should be involved in the audit stage, and considerable support for and opposition to different groups. There is no definitive answer to this question but it is important to raise a number of issues and possibilities.

The Issues

There are reasons why the involvement of others in the audit stage of development planning is very important.

First, the fact that schools are increasingly held to be publicly accountable suggests that they would be wise to involve some of those to whom they are accountable in the formulation of their priorities and targets.

Second, the existence and likely increase of open enrolment suggests that schools will need to show parents and others how they are achieving certain targets and how they take into account the views of parents.

Third, if the audit stage is to provide a description of the whole school, some of the key areas it reviews (see Section 1.4) are concerned with matters external to the school. The school constituency would be a good example of such an area. It is difficult to see how the school can accurately gauge its strengths and weaknesses at dealing with its constituency unless it involves some of that constituency in the audit process.

Fourth, one of the dangers of leaving the development planning process entirely to the staff of the school is that there is an inevitable risk of the staff becoming victims of their own institutional culture. An external view can help.

Fifth, despite the introduction of devolved management, the headteacher and staff of a school are not unilaterally responsible for what goes on there. While the governing bodies of most schools now have considerable responsibilities and powers, the local authority still has some influence, not least in the monitoring and inspection of those schools.

In fact, the list of those, other than the staff, who have a legitimate interest in the devising of a school development plan could be quite lengthy. It can easily include

- the governing body
- parents
- local inspectorate
- HMI
- DES

- LEA
- the local community
- 'feeder' and/or 'receiving' schools.

Given those responsibilities and that interest it seems not unreasonable that they might take an appropriate part in the process.

Involvement in practice

All of these arguments seem reasonable to us and we think schools should make a commitment to appropriately involving others in the audit stage as soon as possible.

We have already mentioned how some schools fail to maximise the potential of school development planning by rushing into the process without considering whether the context of their school is the right one. We can't over-estimate the dangers of this; we need to remind ourselves constantly that poorly managed development planning contains the seeds of its own destruction. If that is true among the staff group of a school then it is doubly true of the involvement of other groups.

Although we believe all schools should make a commitment to involving others in the audit stage, we also think it important to go through the same process with, for example, governors and parents, that you went through with your own colleagues.

- Are the governors and parents ready to be involved?
- Do they understand what school development planning is?
- Are they aware of the problems which badly handled auditing can create?
- Are the staff at a stage where they need to 'practise' on their own or are they ready to involve others?

So 'involving others as soon as possible' means when their contributions will be most productive. Like most of the difficult decisions involved in development planning this can be an excuse for deferring involvement almost indefinitely. We prefer to see it differently – as a way of introducing the involvement of others at the most useful and productive moment.

We mentioned another qualification – that of ensuring that the involvement was 'appropriate'.

A commitment to involving others doesn't mean that they all need to be involved across each of the six key areas or at the same level of intensity as the staff or as each other. As we know from our own experience, being involved inappropriately is as demoralising as not being involved at all.

We need, therefore, to define what the most appropriate involvement in the audit stage is for the various groups with whom we have to deal. Again, these decisions must reflect the context in which you work and it is difficult to give definitive answers. The following comments were made to us by headteachers and teachers who are committed to involving others. We hope they are useful in indicating when involvement might be appropriate and when it might not.

"We were sure there were ways we could improve communication with parents but we weren't sure what they wanted. We asked a group of them to give us their views".

"We went and talked to the local shopkeepers to ask how our children seemed to them after school. Apart from the one or two terrors we knew about we were pleasantly surprised by their response."

"We suspected that our communication systems in school weren't as effective as they should have been. We invited an outside consultant to come in and have a look for us. People opened up to him in a way they wouldn't with me – particularly as I seemed to be the stumbling block!"

"Our governors were very keen to have an input into some of our policies but they didn't want to know about our day-to-day teaching. They simply felt they didn't know enough to comment."

There is no one way in which the audit should take place and over the past few years a number of different approaches have been suggested. We shall provide examples of three of these and outline their strengths and weaknesses in the next few pages.

Whichever approach you choose – and it is has to be the one which suits your context and meets your needs most closely – it will not be perfect. What is important is that the approach should meet the basic principles of the audit stage. What are those principles?

1 Keep in mind the purpose of the audit

The audit is a review of where the school is now – a description of its strengths and weaknesses as perceived by those connected with it. This statement will be precise in some areas, less precise in others. You may, for example, want to describe the children's performance in mathematics statistically, following the use of a test of some description, but you may also want to describe their attitude towards mathematics much more subjectively.

Each of the six key areas is capable of being described similarly, although some are more likely to be described informally rather than formally. Whichever you decide, it is important to understand what the audit is meant to do.

2 Strike a balance between self-justification and self-flagellation

Try to ensure that the audit stage neither becomes an exercise in self-congratulation, nor an exercise in permanent self-criticism. The declaration of strengths and weaknesses is the crucial outcome; try to ensure that both are based on some realistic evidence.

3 Emphasise the strengths as well as the weaknesses

When schools and colleagues are under pressure, as many of them are now, it is all easy to concentrate on the weaknesses which have been revealed and forget about the strengths that exist. Think of the end of an open evening where it seems impossible to ignore the one difficult parent we have just seen even when the other twenty-nine were all pleased with the progress their children were making.

Something similar can happen at the end of the audit stage. Try to make sure that the successes are valued and celebrated before the weaknesses are looked at, with a view to defining priorities. It is important that everyone should share in the good things that are going on.

4 Make sure all of the six key areas are covered

We said earlier that it doesn't matter whether you use the key area headings we have recommended. What does matter, is that your audit has covered everything you feel to be important about your school. The six key areas are an effective aide-memoire to that.

5 Appreciate the need to involve others

Effective school development planning isn't a top-down process, but one which involves everyone playing an appropriate part. This isn't to say that the headteacher and/or the senior management team shouldn't have a final 'editorial' role within the whole process; we'll have something to say about the role of the head towards the end of the book.

What it does mean is that everyone in the process must be given a chance to be involved at a level appropriate to their experience and interest. Once again, this means that some professional judgement has to be exercised as to what these levels are, which requires sensitive handling. Too little involvement from those with something to contribute can lead to disenchantment; too much involvement can do the same.

In the DES booklet *Planning for School Development*, Hargreaves *et al* suggest a number of possible approaches. These aren't to be seen as directives – what they emphasise is how appropriate involvement might be organised.

*A **curriculum leader** in a primary school leads a small group to scrutinise a selection of pupils' work from different year groups to examine progression and continuity and their relation to the National Curriculum.*

*A **department** in a secondary school reviews its curriculum provision; assesses the implications of the National Curriculum for that subject; analyses policies and practice on pupil assessment; analyses examination/test results; reviews pupils' written work to check on progression and continuity.*

*A **team** considers relations with parents and the wider community.*

*The **head, deputy or a senior teacher** leads a working party on topics such as cross-curricular issues, curriculum provision as a whole, pupil attendance, the school's documentation.*

*The **staff development or INSET co-ordinator** leads a working party to review staff development, INSET provision and dissemination, teacher appraisal, care of probationer teachers.*

6 Take into account the professional and personal lives of those involved

School development planning takes time – time which is valuable to teachers who have class, curriculum and other responsibilities, including their families. Just as it is counter-productive to create a schedule for the audit stage which is so loose that nothing ever gets done, so it is counter-productive to create a schedule or choose a process of auditing which is so time-consuming or so urgent that it breeds frustration among colleagues. If the time schedule is too tight colleagues will either respond in great detail but become frustrated by the time they need to achieve such a response, or respond superficially (to get it all out of the way) and become frustrated later when the school development plan doesn't appear to be benefiting them at all.

One of the important parts of the backstage work required before planning begins is to think of the most appropriate time-scale for your school and your colleagues. A question which should continually be uppermost in your thinking (while still applying a degree of urgency) is, what is the most you can reasonably expect to complete by the end of this term, the next term and the next?

Some of the most successful schools we have worked with have created their own timetable for the early stages of their development plan process and declared that timetable to the staff and others involved. In that way no one is under any illusions about what is required and most people will, hopefully, see the time-scale as reasonable.

Each of the above principles is important in helping this first stage of the process towards a successful and purposeful conclusion. There seems little point in spending an inordinate amount of time choosing the methods by which we will carry out our audit in school if the outcomes are going to be ruined by an inadequate understanding of the principles involved. On the other hand, an understanding of those principles and the willingness to implement them can often make up for the inevitable deficiencies of the tools we use.

We began the previous section by pointing out that a number of different methods for auditing the schools have been devised and tried out over the past few years.

Among these are:

- Lists of questions about the school – as in ILEA's *Keeping The School Under Review*, the Salford *Questionnaire* or Surrey's *Primary School Review*.

- Attempts to devise a full process for school audit or review. Probably the best known of these is the GRIDS system (Guidelines for review and internal development in schools) but more recently David Hargreaves produced a similar, although different, version following his experiences as chief inspector of ILEA.

- The creation of continua to describe an aspect of the school. Rodger and Richardson in their book *Self-Evaluation for Primary Schools* suggested that the staff might look at the climate of a school by deciding where they felt the school fitted on lines which ranged from 'inhibiting'… to …'stimulating', 'rejecting'… to … 'welcoming' and 'dull'… to …'attractive'.

- The use of formal testing to measure appropriate aspects of the school or to use the results of already established testing procedures to stimulate discussion about the strengths and weaknesses of particular curriculum areas.

- The two-question questionnaire. We have seen this work well in a number of schools. Staff are initially asked to simply respond anonymously to two questions for each key area:

- The things we are already doing well in this school are …?

- To make this school even better we should…?

The following pages will show three of these methods in a little more detail and highlight what we see as their relative strengths and weaknesses.

The professional decision which someone in each school has to take is to find the most appropriate method for their purposes and their context. This always results in a trade-off and few people are completely happy or satisfied with their eventual decision. However, something must happen to begin the process; as long as some serious attention has been paid to the choice to be made we simply have to begin somewhere. The choice will inevitably depend on a few important factors.

First, is the method we are using suitable for providing us with the information we need?

Second, are the results we obtain from our chosen method likely to be valid and reliable and, therefore, helpful in determining reasonable targets?

Third, is a reasonable balance likely between the amount of work required by the audit method we choose and the benefits we shall gain from it?

Recently we came across the 80:20 rule or, as it is otherwise known, the 'Pareto Principle'. You may have heard of it. It states that "You can achieve 80 per cent of what you require with only 20 per cent of the available effort. To obtain the other 20 per cent requires 80 per cent of the effort."

This rule applies to much of school development planning and particularly to the audit stage. There seems little point in choosing a method which requires a massive investment in time and energy if the outcomes in comparison are not significantly greater. In the context in which all schools are operating at the moment it seems to us most sensible to choose the method which gives you most of what you want for the most efficient use of your time and energy.

Just occasionally, the 20 per cent your most efficient method fails to give you will be the crucial 20 per cent you need to know. This only goes to prove that no rule is straightforward. Yet again, your professional judgement is required. At the very beginning of school development planning, our advice is to err on the side of caution. If your priorities are arrived at as a result of an inadequate audit you will quickly find dissatisfaction setting in.

1   GRIDS (Guidelines for review and internal development in school)

The model for GRIDS is shown opposite.

The five stages of the internal review and development process

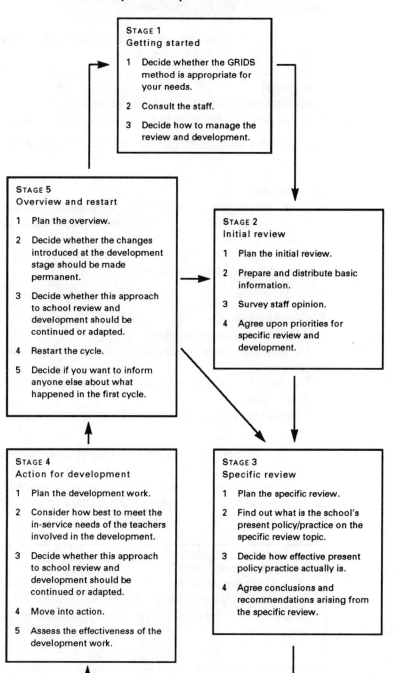

STAGE 1
Getting started

1   Decide whether the GRIDS method is appropriate for your needs.

2   Consult the staff.

3   Decide how to manage the review and development.

STAGE 5
Overview and restart

1   Plan the overview.

2   Decide whether the changes introduced at the development stage should be made permanent.

3   Decide whether this approach to school review and development should be continued or adapted.

4   Restart the cycle.

5   Decide if you want to inform anyone else about what happened in the first cycle.

STAGE 2
Initial review

1   Plan the initial review.

2   Prepare and distribute basic information.

3   Survey staff opinion.

4   Agree upon priorities for specific review and development.

STAGE 4
Action for development

1   Plan the development work.

2   Consider how best to meet the in-service needs of the teachers involved in the development.

3   Decide whether this approach to school review and development should be continued or adapted.

4   Move into action.

5   Assess the effectiveness of the development work.

STAGE 3
Specific review

1   Plan the specific review.

2   Find out what is the school's present policy/practice on the specific review topic.

3   Decide how effective present policy practice actually is.

4   Agree conclusions and recommendations arising from the specific review.

The purpose of GRIDS is to create a systematised review of a school which creates priorities, evaluates those priorities and re-creates new priorities. It does this by recommending

- a general overview of the school to establish broad priorities which then need to be looked at more closely
- a more detailed and specific review of those areas considered important
- development of priorities within those areas
- an assessment of the success achieved in reaching those priorities.

The last two of these, of course, are not concerned with the initial audit.

The strengths
+ The major strength of GRIDS is that it encourages teachers to see development planning as a process and provides help in identifying what that process is. This is not to be devalued.
+ GRIDS is very much school-based. GRIDS can promote a sense of ownership among those who use it.

The weaknesses
- It can be very time consuming.
- The structure it imposes may be too rigid and complex for smaller schools.
- The initial review may not provide sufficient evidence to reveal the priority areas.
- It doesn't allow a great deal of involvement from outsiders.

GRIDS was first published in 1984 by Longmans for the Schools Council and was written by McMahon et al. A revised version was published in 1988. In 1986 a teachers' guide was produced by Peter Holly and published as a Working Paper by the Cambridge Institute of Education.

Comments from user
"The good thing about GRIDS was that it gave us a framework within which to work. Overall we found it too complex, but it reminded us that the need for a framework was crucial."

---

2   Review questionnaires

A number of these have been published. Probably the most widely known of them is *Keeping the Primary School Under Review* published by ILEA in 1983. They all share in common a list of questions which are intended to act as prompts to teachers taking part in a review of their school. They are also wide-ranging. *Keeping the Primary School Under Review*, for example, contains a series of questions about

- the children, their parents, the governors and the community
- teaching organisation, the school staff, responsibility structure, non-teaching staff and staff development
- the curriculum, its continuity and assessment
- school organisation and management
- the building and general environment
- self analysis for the class teacher
- self-analysis for the headteacher
- the future
- the acid test (which is, incidentally, whether you could recommend this school to your friends for their children).

It is impossible to list all of the questions contained within *Keeping the Primary School Under Review* but here is a flavour.

The children

1 Has the school developed policies concerned with
   a) multi-ethnic education?
      What more should be done?
   b) equal opportunities for girls and boys?
      What more should be done?make for:

2 How has the school responded to
   a) Changes in the school role over the previous twelve months?
   b) Levels of attendance? What is the level of absenteeism? Is this higher or lower than last year? What is being done for children who persistently absent themselves from school?

Governors, parents and the community

1a) What contacts are there between the school and its governors?

b) How does the school involve the governors in its life and activities?

c) How does the school involve the governors in the development of its policies?

2 What initiatives are taken to introduce the school to parents? Are these satisfactory?

3 What is done to give parents an understanding of what the school is trying to do?

4 Are parents clear that the school recognises and values the experience and knowledge they have of their children?

The Curriculum

1 What initiatives have been taken and progress made in developing the curriculum during the last twelve months?

2 In considering the needs and interests of individual children, what provision does the school
- able children
- children with learning difficulties
- children with minor sensory and physical disabilities
- children with behaviour problems
- children who have a specific skill or talent
- equality of opportunity for girls and boys
- children for whom English is a second language
- children from different ethnic and cultural backgrounds?

3 To what extent are the needs of all these children met within the following curriculum areas:
- language development
- the development of mathematical skills and concepts
- aesthetic development
- physical development
- religious and moral development
- personal and social development
- opportunities which give practical contexts and applications for the above in such areas as environmental studies/topic work/ science?

Is a range of experiences provided over a period of time?

The strengths
+ It acts as a reminder about the breadth of each school's activities.
+ It enables those involved other than the staff to answer some of the questions.
+ The questions can act as a prompt whichever method of auditing is being used.

The weaknesses
− There are an enormous number of questions, many of which may be inappropriate in different contexts.
− Can be time consuming.
− Can be difficult to identify the main issues from the number of responses received.
− Little help is provided to schools on how to make use of the evidence gathered.
− If the questionnaire-based review is imposed by an LEA it is likely to be carried out superficially by teachers.

Keeping the School Under Review was published in 1982 by the then ILEA Inspectorate. It is only one of a number of such approaches and our comments refer to the approach rather than this version of it in particular.

Comments from user:
"Lists like this certainly remind you of how much there is to do in schools and how complex the whole thing is. They act as good aide-memoires too. The one problem we found is that they can be overpowering. You have to be selective."

---

3 The two-question questionnaire

We mentioned the two-question questionnaire earlier in this section. In practice it looks like this.

The 'Two-question questionnaire' was devised by a headteacher in response to some of the problems he had encountered – particularly in the audit stage – in getting development planning off the ground. Each of the six key areas of development planning have their own similar sheet.

The things we are already doing well in this school are:

To make this school even better we should ...

The strengths
+ It doesn't depend on discussion and can be completed anonymously.
+ It can be relatively quick for staff to complete.
+ Those interested in the school, other than the staff, can take part.
+ It doesn't follow a top-down model but begins from the views of those involved in the life of the school.
+ It reveals areas of broad agreement and disagreement about the school.
+ It covers all of the important areas in the life of the school.

The weaknesses
– All comments appear to be of equal value.
– Some may be based on less information, knowledge and understanding than others.
– It requires someone to co-ordinate the range of views expressed.
– That person needs to have the respect and trust of his/her colleagues.

Comments from user:
"The one big advantage with this method is its simplicity. In the end, it may be a little too simple and I can see us changing it in a couple of years time. But as a way of getting started it's excellent."

Up to now we have been looking at the audit process as a means of internally identifying the strengths and weaknesses of a school. We have suggested that other groups who have an interest in the school may become involved in that process too. This section underlines the need to look outside of the school if the audit is to be really effective.

The strengths and weaknesses of any school are not only those which refer to the enclosed situation within its walls. Strengths and weaknesses also have to be considered against the demands from outside. To concentrate on one at the expense of the other is to produce an inferior and inadequate audit.

Many businesses have failed because they were unable to look outside their own context and realise that the world was changing, that only if they responded to both external and internal demands would they have a chance of survival. In the 1990s schools are no different.

Schools do not exist in isolation but in a structured context which includes both local and national aspects. In devising a school development plan each school needs to take account of this context which will have a considerable bearing on its targets.

The local education authority

The role of education authorities has diminished as that of governing bodies has increased. Yet they still have a considerable degree of interest, influence and expertise. A school needs to be aware of and heed what is happening and what is being said.

A local education authority is responsible for:

- the overall strategy of education provision within its area
- providing funds for education to be carried out
- monitoring the performance of its educational establishments.

The channels of communication vary but include the political, the administrative and the professional – all of which could be formal or informal. In devising a plan a school needs to take into consideration the various arms of the LEA:

- Council members
- the education department
- the inspectorate.

Council members

Although elected members of the council do not in theory have any
individual authority relating to particular schools, they can have
considerable influence. Through their elected office they have a
great deal of contact with local people and organised groups. They
also have influential voting rights at council, committee and sub-
committee level. Even when politically motivated, their individual
or collective views should be regarded as significant. In addition,
their political decisions are of enormous importance, particularly as
they affect the funding of education. In defining priorities and
stating targets schools must not ignore the politicians' own
priorities.

The education department

The education department (or directorate) administer the education
service on behalf of the local education authority. Headed by a Chief
Education Officer or Director of Education, the officers of the
department have a duty to implement the LEA's policies and
discharge many of its duties. The education department can make
certain requirements on schools. These can include forms to be
completed and reports to be written – all within specified time
schedules. The department will also call meetings, organise events
and introduce various other initiatives. All these need to be taken into
consideration when a school is making its own plans. A school which
is aware of a need to update its record-keeping procedures might, for
instance, want to delay any action if it knows the department has
commissioned a study into the same subject.

With the advent of local management of schools it is interesting to
note that schools are having more direct contact with officers from
other departments. On the one hand this gives greater flexibility and
control, but on the other it means extra work and more initiatives of
which we have to be aware.

The inspectorate

Each local education authority has its own education inspectorate. In
some areas this is known as an 'advisory service' (which elsewhere is
used to denote an altogether different function). Each title has its own
vociferous advocates, but everywhere the purpose is to enable the
LEA to carry out its duty to monitor performance. There appears to
be a growing tendency throughout the country for local inspectorates
to review schools in a systematic manner through a regular cycle of

planned visits over a period of two to three years. A school development plan can provide a focus for such a review which, can, in turn, serve to validate the plan. Their reports become public documents which are presented to the education committee and which are also available to schools, governing bodies and parents. The extent to which an inspectorate can require schools to act upon their findings is an interesting debate, but there can be no doubt as to the potential value of their reports to the planning process. An external, professional view of the school can provide valuable recommendations for consideration which can, if appropriate, be incorporated into the school development plan.

The national scene

> *"Schools will need to develop a range of plans as they prepare for the introduction of various reforms. Many will find merit in having a school development plan which draws together all the complementary strands of planning, including the National Curriculum Development Plan."*
>
> DES letter to Chief Education Officers. 17.2.89

It is an interesting paradox that at a time of increasing apparent decentralisation of education, the part played by central government has increased dramatically. While the contribution of central government can at times seem heavy handed, at other times it provides schools with a great deal of help and support. For example, the paragraph we have quoted above provides schools with a legitimate authority to take part in school development planning – to create priorities, to define what will be done and what won't. Not to take advantage of that centrally approved legitimacy to restore some sense of order and control in the management of schools seems like professional suicide.

Schools must, of course, continue to give due weight to any findings of Her Majesty's Inspectorate. In addition there are issues of greatest importance which have an enormous bearing on the targets within a school development plan including the National Curriculum, assessment and appraisal.

National Curriculum

The National Curriculum, overseen by the National Curriculum Council (NCC), is being introduced into schools over a period of several years. This is not something that schools can decide whether or not to adopt, but something which is compulsory for all maintained schools. The timetable for implementation will therefore strongly affect a school's own plans in two ways. First, it imposes targets and schedules which have to be adopted. Second, it influences the degree to which other targets can be selected. The Department of Education and Science is advocating National Curriculum development plans for all schools and has made National Curriculum education support grants to LEAs dependent upon reviews based on such plans.

The National Curriculum

Timetable of Implementation

		KS1	KS2	KS3	KS4
Mathematics and Science	Autumn Term	1989	1990	1989	1992
English	Autumn Term	1989	1990	1990	1992
Technology	Autumn Term	1990	1990	1990	1993
History and Geography	Autumn Term	1991	1991	1991	1994
Art, Music, and PE	Autumn Term	1992	1992	1992	1995
Modern Foreign Language	Autumn Term			1992	1995

KS1 – Key Stage 1 5-7 year olds
KS2 – Key Stage 2 7-11 year olds
KS3 – Key Stage 3 11-14 year olds
KS4 – Key Stage 4 14-16 year olds

From *The National Curriculum – A Guide for Employers*, National Curriculum Council

---

Assessment

Closely linked with the National Curriculum is the introduction of assessment. Based on the recommendations of the Task Group on Assessment and Testing (TGAT) and overseen by the Schools Examination and Assessment Council (SEAC), assessment of all children in the National Curriculum core and foundation subjects is being introduced over a number of years, in accordance to a published timetable. Again this timetable, with its implications for curriculum planning and staff training, is inescapable and imposes a schedule upon each school.

National Curriculum Assessment

When will the foundation subjects be assessed?

			KS1	KS2	KS3	KS4
Mathematics and Science	Introduction	Autumn	1989	1990	1989	1992
	First reported assessment	Summer	1992	1995	1993	1994
English	Introduction	Autumn	1989	1990	1990	1992
	First reported assessment	Summer	1992	1995	1994	1994
Technology	Introduction	Autumn	1990	1990	1990	1993
	First reported assessment	Summer	1993	1995	1994	1995
History and Geography	Introduction	Autumn	1991	1991	1991	1994
	First reported assessment	Summer	1994	1996	1995	1996
Art, Music, and PE	Introduction	Autumn	1992	1992	1992	1992
	First reported assessment	Summer	1995	1997	1996	1994
Provisional						
Modern Foreign Language	Introduction	Autumn			1992	1995
	First reported assessment	Summer			1996	1997

From *NCC News*, National Curriculum Council

Appraisal

> *"Any formal appraisal system should have one overriding purpose:*
> *the improvement of children's education. It should contribute by*
> *promoting the professional development of teachers and by*
> *improving the management of the service"*
>
> Norman Thomas 'A Tool for Improvement' *TES* 6.3.87

The introduction of schemes for teacher appraisal has been fraught
with difficulty. Much of this has been a result of teachers' suspicion,
fuelled by pronouncements about "weeding out incompetent
teachers" and by attempts to link appraisal with salary levels.
Although some local schemes have been in operation for several
years and there have been pilots for a national scheme, compulsory
implementation was postponed by John MacGregor when Secretary
of State. No sooner was he replaced by Kenneth Clarke than it was
re-introduced again, although the format, and to some degree, the
purpose, seemed unclear at the time of writing. Despite the
misgivings, however, a scheme for teacher appraisal could carry great
benefits, both for teachers and for the children they teach.

The introduction of appraisal has a two-fold implication for school
development plans. First, it must be properly planned – with
adequate training, finance, resources and time. Second, appraisal
must link closely with the development plan. Individual targets
must, where appropriate, be part of the corporate plan. There must
be consistency of intention and a recognition of individual
contribution to the whole.

Other initiatives
Other national initiatives which have a bearing on the way in which
schools determine their own priorities include the requirement to
report to parents, access to personal information, charging for
educational activities, local management of schools, and compulsory
competitive tendering.

Each of these needs to be considered when the school undertakes its
audit. The responsibility for identifying these areas of local and national
importance cannot really be left to busy and hard-pressed classroom
teachers. It becomes one of the headteacher's responsibilities to provide
this overview on behalf of everyone involved.

In an ideal world, the result of the audit would provide you at the very least with

- a clear idea of the strengths and weaknesses in the school
- an idea of which of the six key areas needed most attention
- a motivated group of colleagues ready to begin the process of prioritising
- the beginnings of a genuine involvement from some of those concerned about your school but not involved in its day-to-day running.

We have seen this sort of outcome in a number of schools and it is quite thrilling, particularly when colleagues feel that they are beginning to share in the control of their school once more.

Usually when this happens, someone in the schools has been responsible for the backstage work we spoke about earlier, the climate of the school is positive and the conditions needed to support innovation are already there.

For most schools, the outcomes of the audit stage are not so positively wholesome. Sometimes they turn out to be disastrous – the audit has only served to reveal interpersonal conflict, educational disagreement and general dissension. In such cases, the fault for this is often placed firmly at the feet of those colleagues who have just taken part in the process when, in truth, it probably lies with someone who failed to choose the right moment to begin development planning, took little notice of the need for backstage work or rushed staff through it so rapidly that they barely had time to realise what they were doing until it was all over.

In most schools, the response will be somewhere in between these two. You might find, for example

- some colleagues anxious to proceed to the next stage as quickly as possible, while others feel that they need a break
- some colleagues pleased because areas of the school for which they are responsible have been generally valued, while others are displeased or upset because they feel that weaknesses which have been identified represent personal criticism
- some colleagues pleased with an apparently general agreement about the areas they thought were of concern, while others are displeased that something which particularly bothers them has not been mentioned by anyone else

- some colleagues panicking that, despite what has been previously said about prioritising and choosing reasonable targets, there seems to be an impossible amount of extra work ahead.

These responses are examples chosen from our own experiences in schools and go to show that development planning isn't plain sailing, particularly in the early stages.

If you are beginning development planning for the first time you need to bear in mind that, however convinced you are of its worth, your colleagues may only really value it when it has been shown to improve their work and the education children receive. In the early stages they will inevitably be suspicious. If you are restarting the development planning process because a previous attempt wasn't as successful as you had hoped, then remember that some of your colleagues will carry their responses to that failure into the second attempt.

This range of responses is quite normal and it doesn't necessarily signify that the process has begun disastrously. It simply signifies that it has begun.

However, such responses need to be managed like everything else. How can we do that?

1 Accept all responses as genuine

The professional climate of the school is crucial. Responding to criticism and negative feelings personally – as in "Oh, my God, I'm fed up with your wingeing!" – isn't likely to create a model of professionalism.

2 Try to understand where the criticism is coming from

In our experience, most colleagues have responded genuinely throughout the audit and, therefore, their criticisms and fears are often very real to them. We need to understand these individual perspectives. In one school the opposition and negative response from two or three members of staff was found to be because

- one colleague felt that her post of responsibility would be reduced if the priorities were defined in a certain way
- the headteacher had promised one colleague an increased budget for resources, but this seemed likely to be taken away given the results of the audit

- one colleague was already feeling vastly overworked and couldn't face the prospect of anything else on top of her present workload.

None of these fears had a great deal of rational basis and, in the end, none of them came to fruition. Nevertheless, at the time they were all reasonable given individuals' perspectives. The school concerned had a headteacher who understood her staff well; over the couple of weeks between the audit and the second stage of the development planning process she was able to identify the fears and concerns and deal with each of them in a way which meant something to the individual teachers concerned. A headteacher who took a different view could have had much more trouble – and so could the rest of the staff and the whole planning process.

So, at the end of the audit stage

- expect there to be some dissatisfaction as well as some exhilaration
- keep up the backstage work
- deal with the dissatisfaction and worries
- work with the perspectives of colleagues and not against them
- judge the move on to the next stage of development planning carefully. The timing will never be perfect, but you should always look for the best possible moment.

3 Development Planning in Action

Conducting an audit enables the staff of a school to identify those aspects of school life which need attention. Such identification is an essential step on the way to producing a school development plan, but it does not, by itself, result in its production.

It is interesting – and often humbling – to see how many things are perceived as needing to be done. It is also daunting.

Legislation has drastically altered and increased requirements and expectations of schools. This does not only include the enormous volume of education legislation and its knock-on effects, but also other legislation affecting such things as compulsory competitive tendering, local authority finance, data protection, child protection and so on. Keeping abreast of, and responding to, all this takes a mammoth effort on top of the ever-continuing drive to maintain and improve standards of achieve-ment, behaviour and care, and to operate efficiently and effectively.

Starting on a school development plan can be rather like opening Pandora's box. By the time you have taken into consideration national initiatives, LEA initiatives, the events of the school year, the needs identified by each individual member of staff, and suggestions from governors, parents and others, you can be left wondering how it can ever be achieved.

You can't pay attention to everything at once. Attempting to do too much at one time leads to overload and to chaos. Politics has been described as "the art of the possible". Schools need to decide what is possible, what can be realistically achieved.

You also need to recognise that some things cannot be done – at least, not yet. You need to be able to say "Later", or even to say "No".

> "For most schools the list of issues competing for a place among the priorities will be long. Everybody involved in the school will have personal preferences for immediate attention yet a rag-bag of issues brought together does not make a development plan. Some issues are more important or more urgent than others and so have a better claim for immediate attention."
>
> Hargreaves *et al*, *Planning for School Development*

Once an audit has been carried out, the next step is to identify priorities and turn them into realisable targets.

The general areas identified by the audit have to be refined. They have to be translated into more specific terms.

Choosing priorities means looking at the general areas, deciding what actually needs to be done about them, and what can be done. It means deciding what is most important – and therefore in need of immediate or imminent action – and what can be deferred until later.

There is, therefore, a process of refining the focus of attention throughout the audit stage. At first the purpose of the audit is to identify the general strengths and weaknesses of the school. Sometimes, it is suggested that this is done by looking at the aims of the school and seeing how the actual practice of the school matches up to them. Some teachers have found a more realistic approach to be one in which they look at the practice of the school and then see what aims and purposes can be defined from it. Whichever approach you take, you will soon be aware of a number of broad areas within which you need to concentrate.

Having identified those broad areas moves you on to the second stage. Prioritising is the process through which we identify which of the broad areas of concern need tackling first. Prioritising accepts that not everything can be tackled at once.

The third stage involves the creation of effective targets – those more precise descriptions of action which will enable priorities to be met.

How to choose priorities

Each school needs to have a means of determining priorities. This needs to be clear and fair and to result in a plan of action which is realistic, manageable and effective.

Determining priorities for targets is a professional task. It is the responsibility of the headteacher leading a team of professional colleagues. Yet it is something which must – like most other things – be carried out in an atmosphere which is open to the influence of interested non-professionals. It must also be carried out with due regard to the many outside influences and constraints upon the school.

How each school determines its priorities will depend upon its own ethos and management style. This, in turn, will depend on the character, preferences, experience and expertise of its head and other staff, and on its own unique circumstances. There is no one way for a school to determine its own priorities, but it is possible for schools to learn from what has been done elsewhere.

"Plan construction is easier if, from the start, everyone understands how they can contribute. This means clarifying

- *the consultation procedures*
- *the assignment of roles and responsibilities*
- *the means of decision making.*

In some schools new procedures for consultation and decision making may be needed. The task may, especially in larger schools, be undertaken by a group of staff chaired by the head or a group of teachers and governors. Whatever procedure is chosen, account should be taken of the views of all the staff. There is value in including the support staff and bodies such as a school council or a PTA in the consultation. LEA officers are an important source of advice.

Consultation needs to be seen by all those involved as a worthwhile process in which their views are taken seriously. It is unlikely that all the suggestions for priorities can be accommodated within the plan. The head should seek consensus."

Hargreaves *et al, Planning for School Development*

Priority scales

One means of determining priorities is through the use of a priority scale.

Members of a school's staff are asked to list actions which, in their view, need to be taken – largely, but perhaps not exclusively, in order to meet the general needs identified by the audit. The headteacher (or someone else with delegated responsibility) then collates all the suggested actions for distribution to all staff. The list produced in this way will almost certainly need to be arranged under various headings such as the suggested six key areas of curriculum, staffing, the school constituency, building and site, organisational systems and climate (see page 19). It may be that the headteacher will choose to add his or her own suggestions based on recent individual or collective discussions and knowledge of local or national initiatives, influences or pressures.

The list is then given to all staff with a request that each item is marked with a number between 1 and 4 according to a priority scale (see below).

Priority scale

1 very important – to be done within the coming year
2 important – to be done within the coming year if at all possible
3 fairly important – to be done within the next three years
4 not a priority

The headteacher now analyses the responses and produces a draft list of targets. It is possible to employ a strict system of vote-counting or weighting but it is probably better for the headteachers to use their own judgement and common-sense influenced by previous discussions, their unique overview of the situation and what they consider to be realistic. This way it is possible to avoid inconsistencies and impossibilities and the omission of anything which cannot be ignored. (Preparation for compulsory competitive tendering might not figure highly on everybody's list of priorities, for instance, but the headteacher would know that there was no choice.)

The draft list of targets can now be distributed to all staff (and to any others, such as the chairman of governors, who might be involved in the process), for consideration before discussion at a staff meeting. Discussion at the staff meeting can focus on the overall implications of the proposed targets and on their implications for each person individually. They are able to examine the anticipated effect on the school as a whole and on their personal responsibilities. If necessary the list can be amended and revised so that eventually it becomes a document to which everyone feels they can subscribe.

SWOT analysis

Another way of determining priorities is through the use of a SWOT analysis.

SWOT stands for Strengths, Weaknesses, Opportunities and Threats. When the staff of a school is using this approach, they – or a group of them – meet to consider a general area identified through the audit as being in need of attention. Under the leadership of the headteacher (or someone else with delegated responsibility) they first of all 'brainstorm' the school's strengths in that particular area. All suggestions are written down without any prolonged discussion on any one of them. The same process is used for the school's weaknesses. Then attention is turned to any opportunities being presented to the school and finally to any related threats.

Once this has been done, there is an opportunity for more detailed discussion of anything that has been raised, so that suggestions can be explained, expanded or eliminated.

Next there is further brainstorming – this time on action to be taken. There needs to be proposals for actions to build on the strengths, overcome the weaknesses, take the opportunities and minimalise the threats. These proposals are then discussed in some detail so that there is agreement on what is to be done and on when things should be done. Ideally such agreement should be unanimous, but lack of unanimity should not preclude action – and each school will have its own solution in terms of consensus, majority view or final arbiter.

A similar approach is used for each area identified by the audit. It could be that each area will be considered by the full staff or – perhaps in larger schools – that each area will be considered by a separate team which reports back to the full staff for a final decision.

Decisions about priorities are crucial. Making them cannot be left entirely to chance or individual opinion. A degree of rationality is vital.

The rational approach to decision making can be summarised as follows.

a) Determine what you are trying to achieve, by
   • defining the problem
   • clarifying the problem by seeking extra information if necessary
   • specifying what you are trying to achieve (i.e. your objectives)
   • identifying the factors, especially the critical factors, that will constrain your choice of solution
   • specifying the criteria that solutions must fulfil if they are to be acceptable.

b) Generate as many potential solutions as possible.

c) Evaluate each potential solution (i.e. determine the likely outcomes and implications of adopting it).

d) Choose the one which most closely matches the criteria that you have already established.

Guides to rational decision making provide useful hints but they depend on both perfect knowledge and perfect judgement. In reality we have neither and therefore depend on our individual and joint perceptions and values to reach what will, in fact, be a 'best guess' decision.

The priorities you will have created in your development plan reflect the broad areas around which you feel action is necessary. The commitment to work within these broader areas then needs translating into action – the most crucial stage. Creating targets is the next stage in the process.

What is a target?

'Target' is another word linked with 'aims', 'objectives' and 'goals'. These words have been the subject of great discussion and confusion is recent years. Despite the lengthy arguments and the precise and distinct definitions they still tend to be used as if they were interchangeable synonyms. That the confusion exists just as much outside education is shown by the Chancellor of the Exchequer's budget speech in March 1987:

> *"Last year I reaffirmed the aim set out by my predecessor in 1979, to reduce the basic rate of income tax to no more than 25 per cent. That remains my firm objective.*
>
> *However, given my decision to use the greater part of the fiscal scope I now have to reduce the PSBR, that goal cannot be achieved in this budget. I can, however, take a further step towards it, as I did last year."*

In our particular context we think that a target is something which has been identified as needing to be achieved.

Why set targets?

Target setting is a planning mechanism with a number of benefits.

- **Targets identify what has to be done to meet perceived needs.**
  Thus if a school has a perceived need to improve its image in the local community, then targets can be set in order to meet that need.

- **Targets identify priorities.** By setting a target a school is making a statement about what it regards as most important. (It can also make a statement that there are other things which are important but which can wait.)

- **Targets help us make the best use of time and resources.**
  Having stated priorities and identified targets a school can
  concentrate time and resources (including financial resources)
  where they are most needed.

- **Targets help to co-ordinate a school's many activities.** Schools
  are busy places. It is all too easy for the various activities to run
  into each other and clash. A series of targets make it clear what
  has to be done, when, and by whom.

- **Targets give a sense of achievement.** If targets are set carefully
  and wisely they can be accomplished, thus enabling staff to
  recognise – and receive due credit for – their achievements.

- **Targets make it possible to monitor a school's performance.**
  Once targets have been set they can form the criteria against which
  a school can assess its own achievements – and by which it can be
  assessed.

Target statements

The first law of target setting:

KISS

Keep It Short and Simple

Targets have to be stated in language which is quite clear and
succinct so that there is no doubt about what has to be done.
Wherever possible, targets should be stated in such a way as to
identify the level of success on completion. Unfortunately this is not
always as easy in the school situation as it might appear in industry
and commerce.

Eliot Eisner distinguishes between 'instructional' targets and
'expressive' targets (although he uses the word objective instead of
target).

An instructional objective is one in which the outcomes can be
clearly identified and relatively easily measured. Instructional targets

are those more often used in industry but they are also common in schools. Targets such as

- 'Involve more children in sport'
- 'Hold two book fairs'
- 'Buy new storage for the Resource Centre'
- 'Appoint a new member of staff with responsibility for Technology'

are all instructional targets. They define clearly what has to happen and it is easy to measure success.

Unfortunately, for many of us, much of what is important in education cannot be defined in instructional terms. The outcomes are more cloudy, it is more difficult to define what is expected to have achieved success. Such targets are, in Eisner's words, 'expressive'. 'Expressive' and 'instructional' targets can exist side by side. Taking the four instructional targets we identified earlier we might also want to

- 'Increase children's understanding of the need for good health'
- 'Give children a love of literature'
- 'Develop technological understanding throughout the school'

The differences between the two are quite profound. They have implications for the way in which targets are evaluated, for the way job descriptions are defined, for the way success is measured.

There are three basic problems about targets of which we need to be aware.

Because so much of education needs to be defined in expressive terms we often fail to understand how much can be defined instructionally. Instructional targets are clearer, so try to define your targets this way first – and make sure that, in doing so, you make them as precise as possible. An imprecise instructional target is a contradiction in terms.

The second problem occurs when we evaluate the targets. If instructional targets are much harder to define – precisely because they need to be so precise – it is much easier to gain satisfaction from them, because they are so much easier to measure. Expressive targets don't provide that kind of instant gratification – how do we know if, how or when the children in our school have 'developed a love of literature'?   So we have to be particularly careful to ensure that we find some ways, however informal, to let us know that we are at least on the way to reaching our expressive targets.

The temptation – and the pressure – might be to adopt 'success criteria' or 'performance indicators' – in other words, instructional targets – for everything. The danger is of attempting to measure the immeasurable. Some things can be monitored in this way, but by no means everything.

The other problem is of building in failure through setting unrealistic targets. Again this can happen because of an inappropriate emphasis on measurement. 'All children to achieve a reading age equal to or greater than their chronological age' might be a laudable desire but it would be a very unusual set of circumstances in which it could be achieved. 'A majority of children to improve on their previous year's test scores', might be much more realistic and give something to aim at.

Targets can be put to the SPIRO test

S   Is the target **S**pecific?
P   How will **P**erformance be measured?
I   Were staff **I**nvolved in setting the target?
R   Is the target **R**ealistic?
O   Will completion be **O**bservable?

Living with reality

Quite rightly, teachers have high ideals. Yet we also have to live in the real world. There are many things which could be done in schools – and probably even more that should be done – yet when setting targets it is necessary to keep in touch with reality. Sometimes idealism and reality clash, but in school development planning targets represent our statements of those things we will achieve rather than those things to which we aspire.

Targets must be achieveable. They must be based on a degree of commitment. They must be supported by adequate resources. They must be kept under review.

An effective target is one that can be achieved. In the previous section we spoke of the need to define targets very carefully and to understand when a target needs to be defined 'instructionally' and when it needs to be defined 'expressively'.

But many schools still find difficulty achieving their targets even when they are clear about the kinds of targets they are defining.

> *"I began development planning very enthusiastically. When our headteacher explained what it was all about I could see it made sense. The trouble has been that it just hasn't worked out properly. We've started the second development plan with hardly anything new in it at all – it's just catching up on everything we didn't do last year."*

Almost all the schools with which we have worked have suffered from this problem in the early stages. At its simplest, the problem is that things always take longer than we estimate – or perhaps, that we are not very good at estimating how long things will take.

It requires considerable discipline not only to work out how long it is likely to take to reach a target but also to accept the implications of that decision.

> *"When I came here, it was so different from my last school. There, we were always rushing around trying to do ten things at once. When I came here, the headteacher and I discussed the importance of sorting out all of the resources to teach National Curriculum English effectively throughout the school. I asked him what else he wanted me to do in the first term, but he insisted that was enough. I wasn't used to this way of working – I wanted more things to do.*
>
> *He called me into his office one day after school and pointed out that it meant identifying everything we already had in school, deciding what was useful and what wasn't, purchasing any replacement stock, classifying everything and storing it so that it could be easily used by everyone else on the staff. He actually said that if I could get that done by Christmas it would be really something.*

> *Well, I did get it done, simply because it was all I had to concentrate on – and, for the first time in my career, I actually felt I had done something well enough to be of real benefit to everyone.*
>
> *Since I came here, my job description looks as though I do much less than in my other schools, but I actually get more things done – and done much better."*

The school in which this teacher went to work was in its third year of development planning. Through often unproductive experience, the headteacher and staff had learnt that well-written targets were unlikely to be achieved unless real notice was taken of the amount of time necessary for their achievement.

In these complex times we have to face up to an important question:

> Do we want to have plenty
> of targets and fail, or
> fewer targets and succeed?

School development planning is about success. It isn't about creating an impressive list of targets which can't be achieved. How can we work towards achieving a realistic understanding of the time it takes to achieve each target?

1   Link targets and job descriptions closely

In order to discuss them more easily we have dealt with targets and job descriptions in separate sections, but they need to be closely linked in the formulation of your development plans. Having decided your priority areas for the year – National Curriculum history, for example, or improving communications with parents – you will then need to define exactly what aspects of history or parental communication you are going to tackle. These will be your targets. You might decide, as we discussed earlier, to enable all staff to become familiar with the demands of National Curriculum history or to look at the written communication which goes out from the school.

These targets then have to be turned into action statements – what someone in school will actually do to achieve these targets. These action statements represent the job descriptions.

Before the targets and job descriptions become enshrined in the development plan it is important to take an overview of the whole situation and ask a number of questions.

- How much time will it realistically take for the job description to be done well?
- Given all the other targets and job descriptions covering the six key areas, is there enough time in the term or the year to realistically achieve everything we hope to?
- Given that class teaching is still the major responsibility of teachers in the school, are they being overloaded by the number of targets we have identified?

For many schools in the early stages of development planning the answers to these questions will be uncomfortable – it will become very clear that there isn't really enough time or that everyone will be far too overloaded.

There are simple alternatives available. Either you can press on regardless, hoping that it will work out all right in the end. (It won't, of course. You won't achieve much success, everyone will become ragged and tired, and development planning will be seen as another intrusion into an already hectic world.)

Or you can go back to your original list of targets and refine it. Decide what it is really most important for you to do in each of the six key areas, look at the job descriptions which describe the action necessary and only choose those targets which can be achieved in the time you have available.

This method does work – but, in these busy times, taking the step requires a sort of bravery. Don't be afraid to take it.

2 Don't forget the crises

Even when schools have worked out the time it will take to achieve each target there have still been problems, usually caused by crises.

Schools always have crises: members of staff who leave; outbreaks of illness; sudden and inescapable demands from the LEA or the DES; fund-raising events to arrange, and so on.

Space for these crises needs to be taken into account into the time planning of your development plan. In general, the rule we have found most useful is

> Only plan to fill 80 per cent of the time you have available

In this way you know you'll have some space available for the unexpected – and if the unexpected doesn't materialise you have more time available to either celebrate your successes or to introduce another target you feel to be important.

Setting realistic targets is all about defining them as precisely as possible, working out the action needed via the job description and making sure that the action can be accomplished in the time available. Even then, you won't always succeed – but you'll be improving your chances enormously.

Many of the priorities and targets identified through development planning will require resourcing if they are to be effectively achieved. Resourcing usually means money. Understanding the relationship between finance and your development plan is crucial.

The legislation for the local management of schools (LMS) is introducing formula-funding to all maintained primary schools, which means that their financial allocations are being based on locally determined criteria – largely concerned with the number and age of pupils on roll. It also means that they will have the responsibility of controlling their own budget. This has enormous implications for the preparation of development plans.

Although this is not the place for a full investigation of LMS and its impact on primary schools, we will deal with some of the issues relating to budget preparation as they relate to development plans.

Hargreaves et al suggest four processes in development planning. The first of these is the audit in which a school reviews its strengths and weaknesses. One aspect of the school to be audited is the resources.

Auditing resources

The governors and headteacher need to ensure an appropriate match between plans for development and the use of resources. A development plan needs to be supported by financial and resource planning. This task will become more important as many schools become responsible for their budgets.

Account needs to be taken of

- how and why the school used its resources during the previous year
- how the school judges and ensures effective and efficient use of resources
- how development planning should fashion the use of resources rather than being fashioned by them at a late stage.

Effective auditing of resources will make construction of the plan easier and more realistic. During the audit a person or group should make use of existing information, or gather information, about the deployment of resources between years and budget headings. This involves considering

- the use made of the expertise and time of teachers and support staff
- expenditure on materials, consumables and equipment
- running costs such as heating, lighting, telephone bills
- the use of resources from outside the school's immediate budget
- resources or income the school has generated (and may be able to generate) for itself
- the use of accommodation.

Historical budgeting

The usual way in which school budgets have been formulated before the introduction of LMS has been on an historical basis. Each year the headteacher or whoever is responsible for drawing up the school budget has looked at the previous year's expenditure and replicated that with an allowance for inflation or other known variations.

The major advantage of such a system is stability. Everyone knows where they stand and tried and tested values are put into play. Another advantage is simplicity. There are no complicated procedures and calculations to be employed.

There are considerable disadvantages, however. First of all, the introduction of formula funding means that money is no longer allocated on an historical basis. Even with the transitional period allowed by the LMS regulations there may be a great difference between what used to be allocated and what will be allocated in the future. Furthermore with so much emphasis on 'age-weighted pupil units' it is quite possible for there to be notable variations from year to year.

Second, financial delegation will mean that schools will be responsible for much greater sums of money. Instead of having a few thousand pounds at their discretion they will have hundreds of thousands. Much of this money (probably in the region of 75 to 80 per cent) will be taken up by staffing costs, with tremendous variations caused by incremental points. The budget can no longer be simple and much more attention needs to be paid to needs allocation as opposed to historical allocation.

A third disadvantage of historical budgeting is the lack of ability to respond to priorities identified in a school development plan. If action is to be taken in any particular area, money will have to be found to pay for it. This money may not be available on an historical basis. There are a number of variations on the historical budgeting model.

The first still uses historical expenditure as the starting point. This is then compared with known, calculated and estimated commitments such as salaries, rates, energy costs and cleaning. Adjustments are made and any shortfall or surplus dealt with by moving money around until the calculations all balance.

A second variation takes into account areas highlighted for action under the school development plan. When adjustments are made and moneys moved, extra amounts are allocated as they are available to those areas.

These variations are likely to be attractive to schools in the early years of financial delegation. They allow for continuity from a previous form of budgeting and keep the process relatively simple while providing for a degree of responsiveness to change and to perceived needs. Nevertheless they still result in a process which is rather ad hoc and which does not lend itself to detailed costing of planned activities.

Budgeting by bids

Many schools have, in the past, operated a rather crude form of budgeting by bids. Typically those schools have had no formal budgets at the beginning of a financial year. Then during the course of the year individual members of staff have made requests for books and equipment – either for their own classrooms or for their areas of responsibility. These requests have been considered by the headteacher who has either accepted them in whole or in part or else rejected them.

More sophisticated versions of this approach have emerged in recent years. These have perhaps been prompted by the fact that the DES has been inviting local education authorities to bid for certain resources (such as education support grants) and LEAs have, in turn, invited schools to bid for some services (such as in-service training or computer equipment). Typically a school starts the budget process by allocating funds for known and anticipated commitments. What is left over is then subject to bids. Individual members of staff or staff teams submit bids for sums of money which they believe are required. Money is then allocated in response to the bids.

The advantage of budgeting by bids is that money can be allocated according to need. If the school has a development plan, then bids can be made and answered using that as a basis. Restrictions are not created by what has gone before so there is no artificial barrier to change.

There are disadvantages. One is the lack of consistency. It is in fact difficult to plan if you do not actually know what, if any, financial resources are going to be available. Another is the danger of budgeting becoming a manipulative exercise. People will be tempted to over-bid, asking for a larger amount than required, and hoping to get the lesser amount they need. Money could be allocated to areas whose advocates are more articulate or forceful, leaving other areas underfunded not because of lack of need but because of lack of manipulative skills.

Budgeting by costing

An unusual, but perhaps the most appropriate, way for a primary school to prepare a budget is by costing items on the development plan. An important aspect when devising a plan of action is the cost of implementation. As priorities, targets and actions are considered, attention is paid to the financial and resource implications. When items are included in the plan they are accompanied by detailed costing. These costings then form the basis of budget allocations. The actual allocations either take place at the same time as the plan is drawn up or at a later date.

Such a process has its disadvantages. It is time-consuming and complex, calling for skills which might not be readily available in a school. It can also highlight any lack of funding by precluding necessary activities taking place because of lack of resources.

The principal advantage of budgeting by costing is that funds are allocated by agreement and on the basis of identified need. The development plan takes central place in the management of a school and the financial procedures serve the plan.

It is unlikely that schools will be able to immediately adopt this approach to budgeting. It is, however, an approach that many schools will want to aim for at some time in the future.

A problem facing schools when trying to integrate school

development plans with budgetary plans is the discrepancy between the school year and the financial year. If a development plan covers the school year then it comes into operation when the existing financial year is five months old and the next one seven months away.

There are various ways of dealing with this, none of them satisfactory.

- Have a school development plan which covers financial years.
- Hold allocations back until the beginning of the school year.
- Make provisional allocations in September and revise them in April.
- Make provisional allocations in April and revise them in September.
- Plan well in advance so that plans can be put into operation when the money becomes available.

In reality schools use and will continue to use budgetary processes which are an amalgam of various different styles. What they do depends on individual preferences, perceptions, skills and situations. It also depends on the financial resources available to them.

What is important, though, is that all available resources are used to support the school development plan which is an agreed statement of perceived needs, targets and activities intended to improve the education of children.

Who does what?

One of the most difficult problems for many schools involved in school development planning is translating the plan into action – actually making something happen. It is also one of the most crucial.

We need to continually remind ourselves that development planning is not only about devising a formal plan which represents the analytical processes the staff and others have been through, however important and necessary such a written document may be. The success lies in the positive action which results from it, action which improves the school in a number of ways and which affects the quality of education the children in the school receive.

This doesn't only mean improving curriculum policies. Important though they are, we know that in most schools the execution of those policies is affected by interpersonal relationships, the climate of the school, the organisational systems and so on. That is why the most effective development planning covers the six key areas we have talked about earlier. All of them can make a positive contribution towards improving the education of children.

So how do we make the leap from a series of carefully thought out, written-down priorities into action? In the beginning, by understanding that those priorities need translating into activities people will do to bring about their achievement. These activities are described in job descriptions.

What does a job description do?

- **It lets people know what is expected of them.** This means that the language of job descriptions needs to be as precise as possible. 'Sort out the Resource Centre during the next academic year' isn't really satisfactory – any number of actions could result from this. 'Reorganise all charts, videos and slides so that they support the cross-curricular themes chosen to meet the National Curriculum' is a little better.

- **It allows people to know when they have succeeded.** One of the dissatisfactions of working as a teacher is the feeling that there is always something else to be done. Most of us have felt at the end of a school year that there are a group of children in our class who really haven't progressed as much as we would like; that our own professional development and understanding isn't as great as we might have hoped; that there is still so much to do in our particular area of responsibility that we are never going to get it finished.

This is the reality of being a teacher and it won't change – there is always more to do. One of the cumulative effects of this is that we lose the feeling of having achieved anything, of being able to celebrate success. In the present climate we need to restore the celebration of success as much as possible. Well constructed realistic job descriptions can help to do this.

- **It provides a framework for professional, rather than personal, debate.** A good job description – arrived at after serious consideration of the school's needs and each colleague's abilities, time constraints and other responsibilities and agreed by both the head-teacher and the post-holder – provides a framework around which discussion of professional development and professional performance can take place. In too many schools post-holders and head-teachers have had to construct discussions and form opinions about each other in a vacuum filled only by personal opinion and interpretation. Well constructed job descriptions can help to neutralise some of the personal difficulties which inevitably result. This becomes particularly relevant as and when appraisal is introduced into schools.

- **It provides evidence across the school about who is responsible for contributing towards the prioritised targets.** The existence of targets is essential but they don't begin to answer the question from inspectors, governors and others which says 'How are you moving towards this target?' The existence of job descriptions in a school provides some evidence that action has been thought about.

These are all positive advantages. However, we shouldn't get carried away by assuming that the existence of job descriptions guarantees that positive action will take place. Badly managed job descriptions can

- create mistrust – 'Is the only way you trust me to do anything to write it down?'
- create demarcation disputes – 'It's not my job to do that. Look at my job description. Where does it ask me to do that?'
- create friction – 'There's a lot more in my job description than in Fred's. What's he doing to earn his money?'
- create distress – 'You mean I've got to take on board sorting out resources for teaching history? I don't know anything about teaching history!'

These potential problems need careful thought. The process of school development planning is about identifying strengths and weaknesses – supporting the strengths, prioritising which of the weaknesses need attention, defining targets, creating action towards those targets and evaluating what has been achieved. Job descriptions are an important part of that process and need to be developed.

But they don't make it happen; they simply describe what is supposed to happen. Making the job description active is a process which is dependent upon effective management, on understanding the abilities of each post-holder, of creating an environment within which that post-holder can work to the best of his or her ability and of ensuring that the post-holder is committed to the targets they are supposed to be working towards. That is why our model of the development planning process on page 18 shows 'implementation' at its centre; it is why *Planning for School Development* by Hargreaves *et al* stresses the importance of the management of the process if the greatest success is to be achieved.

Job descriptions are an important stage in moving from the carefully prioritised targets of your development plan to the achievement of those targets. There needs to be an effective link between each target and the job descriptions which result from them. If a development plan is to have a chance of success we need to make sure that, whatever else we do in school, a substantial part of our efforts should be directed towards the specific targets identified in the plan.

Let us assume the existence of two agreed targets in a school's development plan. The first says that 'The staff of the school should be familiar with National Curriculum history by the end of this school year'; the second says that 'The School will review and improve its internal communication systems'. How can job descriptions be arrived at from these targets?

1 Check that the targets are clearly understood

Many job descriptions fail because they refer to targets which are imprecise. That is why we spoke earlier of the need to spend time defining and agreeing targets as clearly as possible.

The first target in our two examples does not say that all the staff in the school will begin teaching National Curriculum history; it says that staff will become familiar with it. This has implications for the work which will take place during the year.

The second target, on the other hand, specifically states that more than a review of internal communication will take place. It makes clear that some improvements will be implemented as a result of that review.

2 State as precisely as possible what is required to achieve the target

If job descriptions are to contribute towards improving the school and allow the holder an idea of what it is that represents success, it is important to be clear what has to be done.

In the first of our sample targets, it isn't really enough for the postholder to contribute towards this happening by collecting a few books together and leaving them around the staffroom, attending a course and providing a ten-minute feedback at a staff meeting or cutting out out a few clippings from the *Times Educational*

Supplement. Neither is it enough for post-holders to be allowed to do whatever they want. It would be more helpful for the post-holder to

- provide a breakdown of the history document into its major themes
- organise two staff meetings each term at which a particular area of the document might be explored
- invite an experienced in-service provider with relevant experience of National Curriculum history to some of those meetings
- identify good practice relevant to those areas currently taking place in school.

You don't have to agree with the above statements, only that a job description is only going to be helpful if it clearly identifies what is going to happen.

3 Be clear about the time scales

Many of us in school are notorious for over-planning. It is almost as if we feel that by cramming our lesson plans or our job descriptions to the brim with feverish activity we justify our existence. What usually happens by the end of the year is that we are conscious of how little we have achieved, how much remains to be done and how next year's plans will have to be put back to accommodate the leftover parts of this year.

This lack of clarity about time scales is the enemy of school development planning. If the aim is to create success then we must be sure that our targets and, therefore, the job descriptions which result from them are genuinely capable of being achieved. We need to ask ourselves how long it will take a colleague to review the history document, how much time we can give to the staff meetings (A whole INSET day? Two INSET days? A lunchtime each?) or how long the review of internal communication systems will take.

Only when we are sure that it is achievable within the time constraints we all have does the job description – and the target to which it refers – begin to be useful.

4 The job description should be negotiated

It is rarely ever effective to hand a job description to someone with just the instruction or hope that they will then 'get on with it'. If someone is to be committed to the work they are asked to do, then they have a right to have been involved in the definition of it.

In school development planning this process is helped by the fact that all of the staff will have been involved to a degree in the prioritising of the targets and post-holders and others will, therefore, already have had some input.

That input needs to be continued when the target is broken down into its action statements for the job description. In addition to creating greater ownership of the task, the negotiation of job descriptions respects the fact that the post-holder has some understanding of what is involved in their subject area. The days of one person – usually the headteacher – assuming an all-knowing stance over the entire school are, we hope, disappearing fast.

5 The job description should be within the capabilities of the person holding it

Job descriptions which are beyond the capabilities of the person concerned are pointless. The amount of progress possible is to a large degree defined by the experience and knowledge of the post-holder. So part of the job description may quite rightly refer to the need for personal and professional development as a contribution towards the successful achievement of a particular target. We'll say a little more about this in the next section.

The relationship between targets and job descriptions is an interesting one. Each affects the other in some way. A job description must refer to the prioritised targets contained within the development plan; they are the stimulus to action. But the nature of each target is itself partly defined by what can be achieved within a given time-span by the post-holder.

Creating targets and creating job descriptions are not separate activities. Each responds to and reflects the other.

In the previous section, we suggested that one of the important features of a well-written job description is that it should be within the capabilities of the person holding it. What happens if the needs of the school – as identified within the plan – extend beyond the capabilities of individual members of staff?

Where the school development plan defines priorities and targets which are outside of the capabilities of those in the school there are two options available. The first is to redefine the target to one which is less challenging. While this may be acceptable in some circumstances, it effectively means that the potential development of the school is always restricted by the present – and unchanging – abilities of the staff.

The second option is to build staff development into the plan. This second option potentially allows the school to develop as the capabilities of the staff develop; it is a much more pro-active approach. It is also why 'the staff' has been defined as one of the six key areas of development planning.

A school can only develop as far as the capabilities of those working in it allow. If those capabilities are greater than the school requires at any given moment then the potential for development is built-in. If those capabilities are less than the school requires – and the school is to develop – we have to accept the need for staff development. Three factors need careful consideration.

1 Staff development involves change

Although it is relatively easy to formally describe the staff development which needs to take place, such a description carefully hides the sometimes threatening and often messy context within which   staff development occurs.

For a start, real development takes time. John Harvey Jones points out in *Making it Happen* that

> "Ultimately change is only anchored fully when individuals have changed their perceptions and values and it is important to be realistic about the amount of time this takes. Five years is absolutely par for the course ... and even that is only achievable if one is moving well within the established grain of thinking.'

Now five years seems an awfully long time. Not all the development may take that long, but much that is important will. A change which enables us to understand the demands of different areas of the National Curriculum or the need to improve the way in which everyone in school responds to the community may only take six months; but the change required to actually put those understandings into practice may take a lot longer.

The reasons for this are not difficult to understand – it's just that in the day-to-day rush of running schools they sometimes get forgotten.

Change affects the individuals concerned. It requires all of us to adapt from comfortable ways of behaving to, at least temporarily, uncomfortable ways. It can call into question views and beliefs which have been with us for some time. It makes further demands on us we may not feel like meeting.

Within the context of school development planning, staff development is both necessary for the changes we hope will take place but also a part of those changes, too. It is hardly surprising that it can produce as much resistance as it does support.

2 Staff development has links with appraisal

A formal system of appraisal for teachers has been announced by Kenneth Clarke, the Secretary of State. Quite how the system will operate is, at the time of writing, unclear and we still don't know if the focus of appraisal is to be one linked specifically to staff development or one linked to pay, conditions and disciplinary procedures.

If the first of those alternatives materialises, then a lot of the work which has already been done on how to carry out positive and worthwhile appraisals will be of considerable benefit to the kind of staff development we are talking about here. If the second option materialises, then it will make it much harder for staff development to take place.

Few staff will willingly go through a process where their 'development' is discussed in terms of pay, conditions and their possible future employment, and then go through the same process again with a view to making a contribution towards the positive success of the school development plan. The climates required by each of these approaches are unlikely to be mutually supportive.

3 Staff Development opportunities need to be within the capabilities of each person

Ideally, staff development needs are identified through

- the creation of the school's priorities
- the definition of action needed to support those priorities
- a consideration of the present strengths and weaknesses of those given the responsibility of carrying out the action
- the identification of the support required to address those weaknesses.

If a chain is only as strong as its weakest link, then school development is only as strong as the capabilities of the staff allow. A target which can only be reached by demanding a level of personal and professional development by a colleague which is unlikely to be achieved, is a target which is going to fail.

This suggests that the creation of effective development plans isn't just the identification of targets. The effective development plan is one in which the targets are defined on the basis of their achievability. If staff development is to be a part of a development plan as well as a contributor to it, then the targets set for individual members of staff also need to be achievable within the context of their own personalities, abilities and other demands made upon them.

Only then can staff development have a chance of being effective. Enabling this to happen is at the heart of staff development.

Can staff be 'developed'?

Underpinning the previous section about staff development was the idea that it is a challenging process of change which can have considerable affects upon the individuals involved. John Harvey Jones spoke about individuals changing "their perceptions and values". Jenny Nias goes further than this. She suggests that

> "...teacher development rests on personal development, that the management of change in schools can proceed no faster nor further than the individual's sense of personal identity allows."

What both Harvey Jones and Nias are saying is that development is not something which can be done to people – it is something which people do to themselves. This simple statement has fundamental implications for the process of staff development which arises from the needs of a school development plan. It also explains why the "Send her on a course" method of staff development is such a hit-and-miss affair.

Course attendance can work in effecting change, but only if the person concerned is aware of the need for change, is open and receptive to it and the course meets the needs identified. The success of course attendance, in other words, is only in part due to the course; mostly, it is due to the way in which each individual attending the course responds to it.

The importance of the individual in staff development has at least two important implications.

1 What represents 'staff development'?
We may have too narrow a view of what activities constitute staff development. If a major part of the success of staff development is due to the individual's sense of personal identity, then staff development activities need to concentrate as much on supporting and developing that sense of identity as they do on identifying individual and precise skills which need to be learnt.

We wouldn't want to suggest that such activities shouldn't take place. What we are questioning is the extent to which staff development is usually seen as a purely functional mechanism of increasing skills rather than as a way of enabling the development of the whole person. Inevitably, the two are interconnected, but we shouldn't assume that both will automatically take place.

2 What do staff developers do?

A number of schools have, in recent years, created senior posts for staff development. In our view, one of the dangers of such posts is that they convey the impression that staff development is a top-down model, that in some strange way staff can be 'developed'. Unfortunately, there occasionally seem to be people working in school who seem to believe this, too. "I sent him on the course and he's absolutely no different. What's the matter with him?" (And just in case you think we are making this up, this remark was heard in a school early in 1990.)

Our understanding that effective staff development owes as much to the personal development and commitment of the individual concerned as it does to the existence of formal staff development activities, leads us to believe that the process of staff development is a facilitating one. Anyone assuming some responsibility for staff development needs to concentrate as much on creating the conditions within which people feel able to begin the process of personal and professional development in a relatively safe and unthreatening environment, as they do on identifying development opportunities and sending people on them.

Staff development is a necessary part of school development planning; without it many of the priorities and targets of a development plan will be unachievable. 'Staff developers' can enable it to take place most effectively by

- supporting as much open discussion about and understanding of the prioritised targets as possible
- negotiating – not imposing – the job descriptions describing the actions to be taken
- allowing the post-holder a large part in the negotiation
- negotiating the personal and professional developments identified
- using their 'cool eye' to restrain too much from being taken on by one person (although how much can be taken on will change from person to person)
- leading by example – defining their own personal and professional development and approaching it sensibly

- helping to identify the most appropriate developmental opportunities and not only the most obvious
- supporting both the process of development and the action which results from it
- understanding the lengths of time required for some change to take place
- understanding that most change takes place as a series of small steps rather than giant leaps.

If we follow these steps then we have a good chance of creating a climate within which professional development is seen as normal, positive and possible. In creating such a climate we are beginning the process of achieving some of the targets we have identified as part of our development plan.

What is a team?

William Dyer identifies at least six characteristics of a team in his book *Team Building – Issues and Alternatives.*

- The ability to make sound, free and informed choices or decisions.
- The ability to implement those decisions with commitment.
- A clear understanding and acceptance of the goals (targets) by all team members.
- A climate of trust and support.
- The ability to identify and work through differences between people rather than the willingness to ignore or suppress them.
- An understanding by team members of their roles and how they fit into the overall framework of both the team and the organisation.

Teams, then, are different from groups. In groups, people work together for administrative purposes only; they tend to be less involved in planning the targets; they have less understanding of the roles of others; they are less trusting and so more cautious of revealing what they really believe – and so a real understanding of the situation is less likely.

Are teams better than groups?
Not necessarily. The Henley Management Centre suggests that teams are to be preferred when

> - *people need the comradeship of others*
> - *specialists need a mechanism to co-ordinate their work*
> - *social, not authoritarian methods are needed to maintain standards*
> - *new thinking is needed about problems that are complex enough to benefit from the breadth of input and energy of the group*
> - *collective decisions need to be made*
> - *strengths, weaknesses, opportunities and threats need to be identified.*

In certain situations, therefore, a group is a perfectly acceptable type of organisation. In a school, for example, certain regular procedures can work perfectly effectively in a group context. The handling of registration, the transfer of certain kinds of information or the establishment of some routines such as fire drill don't really need teams at all.

Do all teams work in similar ways?
Yes they do – but what differs is the extent of the collaboration required between team members. Let's assume that a school has devised a policy for the teaching of a particular aspect of the curriculum, has provided and organised the necessary resources to implement that policy and has begun to put that policy into action.

The amount of collaboration required between the team will have changed as the process developed. In the first instance, where the development of the policy required a clear understanding of the needs of the children, the abilities of the staff and the demands made upon the school, a high degree of teamwork was essential.

The organisation of the resources required less teamwork. One or two people could have taken responsibility for this on behalf of the staff; the teamwork occurred in respecting and maintaining that organisation co-operatively.

The implementation of that curriculum policy in the classroom was most likely to be undertaken by individual teachers working with their children or students but without colleagues. The amount of team work which took place at this moment would be quite low; what is required is an acceptance of the team goals by everyone concerned and a willingness to play a part.

We can represent this continuum of team behaviour like this:

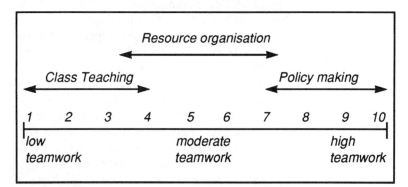

Are teams made up of similar individuals?
No. We highlighted earlier that two characteristics of teams were their ability to work through the differences between people and their usefulness in finding solutions to complex problems.

This means that one of the most important and identifying features of a team is that they contain a range of different people, each of whose contribution is seen as potentially important to the team's activities.

This is seen most clearly in sports teams, of course, but the lessons are often lost in other organisational groups. One of the problems in attempting to create a team is the natural desire to get together people of a similar outlook and temperament – in other words, to create a club of which we are pleased to be a member. Such a group may be comfortable and mutually self-supportive for a while, but it is not best equipped to solve complex problems through a range of different approaches.

Teams respect the individual contributions of team members; they don't insist on uniformity.

The importance of teams to school development planning

If we use the Henley Management Centre criteria for the use of teams you'll see how closely development planning fits with all of them.

- The identification of weaknesses, which is a fundamental part of development planning, is also one of its most threatening aspects. All of us find weaknesses hard to handle and we do so best in an atmosphere in which we have "the comradeship of others to sustain us".
- School development planning is an activity which covers all of the important areas in the life of the school. To work effectively it needs to choose between competing priorities, define appropriate targets, co-ordinate those targets with each other and manage the implementation of them. If this is going to be a success, each person responsible for contributing to that achievement "needs a mechanism to co-ordinate their work".
- School development planning is about the shared understanding and agreement of its targets by the whole staff of a school. Occasionally, it is inevitable that a target will be imposed by external pressures of one kind or another but such imposition of targets is not – from the evidence available – to be recommended as the usual approach. "Social, not authoritarian methods are needed to maintain standards".
- School development planning is, in part, about finding a route through the complex and often ill-defined demands made upon a school. No one person is really capable of defining that route or understanding all of the issues. Such a route is best discovered

through "new thinking" ... benefiting ... "from the breadth of input and energy of the group".

- School development planning is about making "collective decisions" and identifying "strengths, weaknesses, opportunities and threats".

The creation of effective teams is vital to the process of school development planning. In the next section, we'll look briefly at how we can begin to create effective teams.

3.11   Team Building – 2

The development of teams

Teams are a very powerful support to the success of school development planning, but they don't just happen. Just as gathering a collection of footballers together doesn't mean that they will play as a team (even if they understand that this is what they are supposed to do) so gathering a collection of teachers together to work through the process of school development planning doesn't mean that they will work as a team (even if they appreciate the advantages this might bring).

The Five Stages of Team Development – and What Team Leaders Can Do

Stage 1 – Ritual Sniffing

Characterised by: feelings and thoughts being kept hidden; little obvious care for each other; a strict adherence to whatever rules exist; personal weaknesses kept secret; much politeness; lots of words but little listening – or much silence; someone occasionally tries for effect.

What the team leader can do: During this stage it is important that the team leader understands the normality of this situation. We have discussed elsewhere the problems that introducing development planning can bring to both individuals and the organisation. It is unreasonable to expect people to begin the process knowing or understanding what it is all about or showing high levels of commitment to it.

At such times the team leader needs to concentrate on setting the tone, not being disturbed by initial signs of wariness and looking out for the second stage to begin.

Stage 2 – Infighting

Characterised by: the dropping of barriers; the beginnings of a pecking order within the group; the need for each member to establish a role of some sort. If you are lucky and you are working in an already positive climate this can be conflict free. More often, as the debate opens up, conflict occurs around control and dominance of the group and the members' individual values and principles.

What the team leader can do: This is a crucial stage for the team leader who will need to gain the respect of the members of the team. Their individual perspectives need to be understood and their behaviour seen in the light of those perspectives; an openness needs to be maintained so that difficulties and differences are not buried; the team leader needs to be able to deal with cliques and sub-groups which emerge by constantly re-focusing on the common purpose.

Stage 3 – Experimentation

Characterised by: the team learning to work together through their growing understanding of each other; reviews of the performance to date taking place; new methods of working are

Teams have to be developed. One of the most important attributes of the headteacher, head of department or whoever is at the centre of development planning is the ability to understand and respond to the different stages in the growth of a team.

There are any number of ways to describe these stages. We owe a debt to the Henley Management Centre for the five stages described below.

tried; emotional support for the team becomes important; outsiders or the leader being seen as helpful.

What the team leader can do: Help to identify the strengths and weaknesses of the team in relation to their task as uncritically as possible; provide examples of self-evaluation; take on personal self-evaluation of the leadership role publicly and professionally; spot and celebrate successful work; provide an input of new ideas to stimulate and support the reviews taking place.

Stage 4 – Effectiveness

Characterised by: benefits of the work being seen; the team understands its own strengths and weaknesses; the team sees its place in and contribution to the wider organisation; clarity, energy and expertise are utilised to the full; trust develops which increases reliability; often, a pride develops in membership of the team.

What the team leader can do: Often at this stage, there is a temptation for team leaders to sit back and luxuriate in the team's performance. It is important, though, that the leader helps the team to do as well as it can by clarifying and re-affirming the teams objectives; providing the 'cool eye' which overviews everything which is taking place; maximising everyone's contribution.

Stage 5 – Maturity

Characterised by: basic levels of conflict have been dealt with; procedures have been adapted to suit needs; rules are much more fluid; role playing, game playing and pretence usually absent; the leadership role varies from situation to situation.

BUT...there is also a danger that group prejudices can take over and that the team cohesiveness cuts it off from the whole organisation.

What the team leader can do: Be prepared to relinquish the leadership role when it seems appropriate; bring in outsiders to focus the team's perception of itself; keep a look-out for the team closing the doors to other influences.

Remember that this is a model of the stages of team development, not a description of the reality which will always present itself to you. Occasionally, stages will be missed out; occasionally much longer will have to be spent working through one stage than the others.

In a school where "the conditions to support innovation already exist" (Hargreaves et al) the first two stages might already have been resolved by the time school development planning is introduced.

It is possible for school development planning to make some progress without the existence of strong and well-formed teams and, on occasions, the introduction of development planning into a school has created the focus around which team-building can develop. So development planning can be a part of the creation of effective teams.

However, it is also true that the best development planning we have seen has occurred in those schools where teamwork has been seen to be important, has been worked towards and has been highly valued. In those schools, development planning isn't just another contribution to the creation of effective teams – it is one of the arenas in which the effective teamwork which exists can be put to most effective use.

Each of us responds differently to new initiatives. For some the initial impact is very strong, enthusiasm is engendered very quickly along with the willingness to become involved.

For others, the initial impact is much more circumspect; participation is given but evidence of some results is required before real commitment is made.

For others, the full impact of a proposal never really sinks in. Such people never become fully committed but are happy to play a part.

For a few, a new initiative breeds resentment, participation is grudging at best and disappointments are seized upon as evidence of failure.

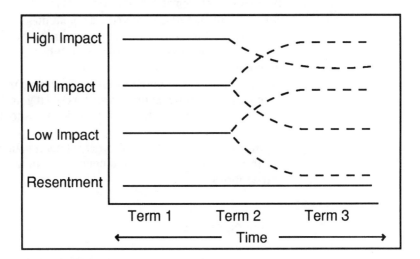

Each response has its strengths and weaknesses. Those with early enthusiasm can often lift a project off the ground; but occasionally this early enthusiasm is re-directed when something apparently more appealing comes up.

Those with initial circumspection can seem like wet blankets at the beginning but, if some success is shown, they can also become the 'engine-room' of a project, deeply committed to it and willing to keep going even when times are tough.

Those never fully committed to an initiative may not generate much excitement, but they are often willing to do their bit when called upon.

Even those who actively oppose an initiative, while interfering with its progress, can cause us to re-examine what we are doing. There is always a chance we have simply been carried away with our own enthusiasm; they may be right!

We need to remember this range of responses when thinking about school development planning.

School development planning isn't something a school does as an additional activity or even as a co-ordinating activity for everything which takes place; it becomes a way of organising the school itself. At its best, school development planning is no less than organising the whole school as effectively as possible.

To achieve this we need to develop a sustained commitment to the process from everyone involved – a commitment which develops out of the range of responses we identified earlier. Any project will move through its high spots and its low spots. When things are going well commitment is hardly questioned; most of us like to be involved in success. But when an initiative hits an inevitable trough, it is the commitment of those involved which keeps it going and which enables the problems to be resolved and success to be regained.

There are any number of reasons why commitment is retained or lost to a project. Some of them are unique to individuals or to particular organisations.

1 Seeing results

It is very difficult to retain commitment to anything which doesn't appear to be delivering at least some of the results we hoped. This isn't unique to development plans – many of us have the same attitude to most aspects of our lives.

It is important that those involved in school development planning should be able to feel that positive results have occurred through the work they have done. We have discussed this implicitly and explicitly throughout the whole book; the ability to define achievable and reasonable targets and job descriptions is crucial to giving the plan a chance of success.

What we have noticed in many schools, though, is that in the rush to do more and more, the successes which have been achieved are not necessarily made clear to everyone. Part of the management of school development planning lies in the identification of success. One of us worked in a school where the senior management team used to set out each day to spot things which were going well. Whatever the failings in that school – and there were a number – the atmosphere was certainly more committed than in schools which only seemed to highlight disaster and failure.

Each day, things will be happening which have some bearing on the successful achievement of the targets within your plan. How many have you identified and made public in the last term?

2 Identifying with the initiative personally

Everyone responds to different things for a range of reasons, some of which are predictable and some of which aren't. If we join a particular music class it may be because

- we have a desperate longing to learn the guitar
- we want to learn an instrument but are not that bothered which
- our social life isn't very good and we want to meet people
- we want to meet a particular someone who also attends the class
- we have dreams of becoming musically famous in a rock-group or in a band
- we can't stand staying in every night
- we can't drive and this is the nearest class
- we hurt our hand a year ago and it needs exercise
- of countless other reasons!

Our commitment to that class is dependent upon how well it meets our real reasons for joining it in the first place. If the organiser wants to keep his class together the worst mistake he or she can make is to blithely assume that everyone is there only because they are desperate to learn the guitar.

The same is true of our commitment to the idea, the process and the targets of school development planning. If we want to develop and sustain commitment we won't do it by assuming that everyone knows that it is a 'good thing' and will therefore happily take part.

Knowing and understanding others means taking the time to understand the perspectives they bring to the particular aspect or aspects of development planning in which they are involved. The more we can ensure that those perspectives are satisfied the greater commitment each person is likely to show.

3 The existence of leadership

For some years now, as ideas of democratic staff involvement have developed, 'leadership' has been out of fashion. But few initiatives can be totally self-sustaining, however positive the results and however much they meet the perspectives of those involved.

Most initiatives need someone to take the responsibility for co-ordinating, for motivating, for accepting the final responsibility; that person is the leader. Effective leadership is an important factor in creating and sustaining commitment to school development planning.

The management of school development planning is a two-way process. We believe it is possible to foster the conditions under which commitment to the processes and outcomes can be engendered; that commitment, in turn, feeds back and contributes to the proceedings.

School development isn't an answer to all of the difficulties of a school. What it does is to establish, through appropriate and co-operative involvement, a series of targets, action steps and review procedures which enable a school to move forward in a more structured, organised and positive way than before.

Within the process things will still go wrong. Colleagues will become disheartened; progress will appear to be slower than one might wish; crises will occur; important targets might have to be put back. The more carefully development planning is managed the less these things are likely to happen, but it can't stop them altogether.

When things go wrong, when the process hits a trough, when it seems unlikely that important targets will be met – then people need support. A school which has already developed a culture in which professional discussion and debate forms a part is likely to be more self-supporting than one which hasn't, but at various times each of the individuals and groups within any school will need an element of support. The danger for a staff or school which identifies itself as being mutually self-supportive is that of missing the key moments when support is really needed.

Support doesn't just happen; it has to be thought about. We'd like to identify four factors which we think are important.

1 Accept the lack of a smooth path

Part of the way we can provide support is in the climate we create around each initiative which is introduced. Experience tells us that things don't go smoothly but sometimes we seem only to be aware of this in theory and not in practice.

This is particularly true when we are responsible for or committed to a particular project. Our desire for it to succeed breeds frustration when things start to go wrong. That frustration then causes us to behave in ways which are not conducive to providing support for all of those involved. We show our irritation; we apportion blame too quickly; we adopt a doom-scenario that 'all is finished'.

These reactions cause an equal reaction in those who are working with us. Occasionally that response is a positive one and people work harder to support us. More often than not – and especially when people are under pressure – the response becomes even more negative. Less gets done and the climate degenerates.

Yet all the time, we know that this is how things happen. We need to move this perspective from the back of our minds to the front. Accepting that there will be the occasional disaster allows us to choose realistic time scales within which people can work, allows people to feel better when things do go wrong and, most importantly, creates a climate of reality which supports what school development planning is all about.

2 Highlight potential difficulties

Once we have publicly accepted that things will go wrong – and are seen to genuinely accept this – then we can begin to try and identify some of the possibilities before they happen. This creates further reassurance that not everything is expected to go smoothly; it also enables a certain amount of preparation to take place which minimises the disturbance caused.

In an earlier section about job descriptions, we identified the possibility that part of a job description for one year might be to organise two staff meetings a term in which staff could discuss and become familiar with the National Curriculum History document. We know that in most primary schools the four weeks leading up to Christmas are fraught with interruptions and that the last few weeks of the summer term can be taken up with report writing, open evenings, sports days and the summer fair.

Identifying these ahead of time should help us to organise those two staff meetings at a time when they support our colleagues rather than interfere with and make worse their already overloaded schedule. This sounds simplistic. Yet one of the authors, in his early days of headship, was actually responsible for introducing the work of a team of colleagues to the rest of the staff on a hot June evening on the day after Sports Day. This was not felt to be a positive act by those colleagues on the receiving end; not unnaturally, they withdrew much of their support. The resulting bad feeling meant that a moratorium was declared on curriculum meetings for a term.

Equally, identifying and making public potential difficulties enables everyone to at least prepare themselves for their arrival. If we know there is a likelihood of something happening, it can seem less of a disaster when it actually happens.

Of course, making public likely difficulties has to be handled sensitively and in the context of a forward-looking and dynamic overall plan. Otherwise the identification of difficulties simply becomes an excuse for standing still!

3 Look for the 'approximately rights'

If we can accept that the progress of our overall development plan is unlikely to go smoothly then we need also to accept that the progress of each of our individual contributions to that plan might not always go smoothly either.

The view we have about this has an effect upon the way in which we recognise success in our school and the way in which we are able to support ourselves and colleagues honestly. The One-Minute Manager provides a reminder which is both realistic and useful:

> *"In the beginning, when working on performance, you need to set things up so you can catch people doing things approximately right (short term goal), not exactly right (final goal) ... The journey to exactly right is made up of a whole series of approximately rights."*

The idea of identifying 'approximately rights' is a very reassuring and, ultimately, a very supportive one. We need to have our own definition of what 'approximately' means, of course. Too loose, and we find ourselves supporting 'achievements' which are hardly achievements at all. Too tight, and we find ourselves with hardly anything to support.

Nevertheless, it is important that we carry our understanding of the complexity of what we are doing with us. Only then, can we really give people the support they deserve.

Many, although not all, the initiatives which schools have had to respond to over the past few years have, individually, been of value. The problem has been in the management of their introduction. Too many at one time, little clarity about what they mean, changes of rules half way through and only grudging thanks for the profession's attempts to come to terms with any of them. It is an irony of some proportions that to study the work of the DES and many recent ministers at the department is to construct a self-taught course on how not to implement school development planning in your school. It is an even bigger irony – which doesn't appear to have struck the department – that effective development planning for schools is now a part of their recommendations. It is hardly surprising that one occasionally wishes that they had read and taken notice of their own documentation.

The result of all these initiatives is that schools and teachers have found themselves on a treadmill. In the two months preceding the writing of this book we heard in various staffrooms across the country expressions such as

"I remember when I used to look forward to walking into school in the morning, but now…"

"We used to have time for a laugh, but now, it's just meetings, meetings, meetings."

The number of teachers who are either leaving the profession or thinking of leaving it is further witness to the dissatisfaction felt by many. Despite considerable attempts by many to respond as well as they can, the idea of celebrating the success which has been achieved seems to have been lost in the day-to-day vocabulary of schools.

For us, this represents one of the biggest disappointments of the past few years. Celebration is the way in which we restore our energies, regroup and reassure ourselves that something positive is happening. Achievement without celebration is hardly achievement at all.

We have seen earlier how well-managed school development planning should lead towards more success by identifying clear priorities, by creating achievable targets, by defining realistic job descriptions and by evaluating their success. In the previous section we emphasised the reality of looking for – and identifying – the 'approximately rights' that we found.

But identifying those 'approximately rights' is not always enough. Sometimes a school needs to celebrate its successes.

The way we celebrate will depend on the kind of school we work in and the nature of the people we work with. There's no point having a wine and cheese evening after school if everyone is teetotal; there is no point booking tickets to a musical if everyone is tone-deaf. Each celebration needs to be carefully chosen to meet the context within which it is going to take place.

There are numerous ways in which celebrations can take place. They don't all cost money and they aren't all very glamorous. They are important, however, and some of the best schools we have worked with are not only successful in the management of their development planning, they are also successful in celebrating it.

To give you some idea of what we mean by celebrations, we have worked with schools which have

- bought a particularly welcome piece of equipment when – and only when – a major target has been reached
- cancelled after-school meetings for a month
- provided flowers for every classroom as a special thank you
- organised theatre visits for the staff
- had an after-school wine-tasting for the staff
- reserved a small amount in the budget for distribution to staff to spend on their classroom
- produced a special edition of the school newsletter for distribution to parents
- held an INSET day at a very luxurious hotel, so its facilities could be enjoyed to the full once the day was over.

Some of these are possible in every school – the biggest difficulty for some schools is convincing themselves that they are possible. If a part of school development planning is about helping schools become pro-active again, then a part of that pro-activity is to realise how much the occasional celebration is a part of every successful organisation's well-being.

Schools may not be able to afford some of the corporate hospitality or generous gifts of some of the largest private companies, but we can all share in the same principle and do what we can. After all, we deserve it.

Creating a Format – The General Issues

A question that is usually asked when schools begin the process of devising a school development plan is "What does one look like?" There is no straight answer to that question because there is no one format which is universally acceptable. Generally speaking it is for each school to design its own format to suit its own unique position.

> *"Many schools believe that they would profit from seeing examples of real development plans. This can be valuable, but there is no standard or 'model' development plan. Each school has its own history and culture from which its unique plan arises."*
>
> Hargreaves *et al, Planning for School Development*

The need for an agreed format

In one sense the actual format of a plan is the least important aspect of the whole process. What is important is the evaluation of the situation, determining priorities and targets, putting them into action, and then reviewing progress. It might be argued that besides all this, how – and indeed if – the procedure is set down on paper, is of little significance.

The format of a school development plan can, however, be crucial. An agreed format is important for many reasons.

- **It demonstrates involvement.**
  Staff need to have a sense of ownership of the planned development and, where possible, governors and parents need to feel that they have contributed. The very fact that a format is agreed is a demonstration of the involvement of the people who agreed it. It shows a recognition of the uniqueness of the school and the way in which individual skills and perceptions are valued. Although it may seem easier to take a format 'off the peg', to do so without considering alternatives is to risk the impression of imposition and the loss of something better. Some LEAs have, it seems, set down a required format for schools to follow. They have done this to ensure that plans are made and/or to allow for commonality in practice to facilitate reviews by inspectors. The danger is that 'development' becomes a paper exercise with no real commitment.

- **It provides a focus for action.**
  Most primary schools are fairly small organisations in terms of staff numbers. It might be a fair assumption that with full

involvement, and what Peters and Waterman have called "a bias for action", that everyone has a clear view of what is intended. Yet clear views tend to become blurred with the passing of time. We too often find that, despite good intentions, we have, in the words of the prayer book, "left undone those things which we ought to have done, and we have done those things which we ought not to have done." An appropriate agreed format helps to ensure that the right things are done at the right time. It does, in fact, put individual members of staff in quite a strong position as it makes clear what is expected of them. They can plan ahead and can reasonably expect not to have surprises thrust upon them.

- **It provides a means of presenting the plan.**
  There are others besides the school staff who have a legitimate interest in a development plan. Governors have a responsibility to see that a school is being properly managed and the children properly taught. Parents have a responsibility to make informed judgements on which to base decisions on their children's education. LEAs have a responsibility to monitor provision and performance. They can all be assisted in meeting these responsibilities by access to a school's development plan in an appropriate agreed format. Schools might, however, feel that they are exposing themselves to criticism by publicising their own weaknesses. In reality it can be used to ward off any criticism as the message is: "We are aware of our strengths and this is how we are going to build on them. We are aware of our weaknesses and this is how we are going to overcome them."

- **It provides a means of assessing progress.**
  By committing to paper what has to be done, a school provides itself with a way of recording its own success. At the very least a format can be regarded as a checklist on which activities can be ticked off as they are completed. At best it supplies a school with its own performance indicators – setting objectives to be achieved and recorded. A format which contains realistic targets within a defined timescale encourages and nurtures success by giving something to aim for and then celebrating achievement. It can also act as a record for others – inspectors, for instance – of what was intended and what has actually been done.

Criteria for formats

In designing and agreeing a format for a school development plan there are a number of factors which need to be taken into consideration.

- **The format should contain realistic targets.**
  The targets contained in a development plan need to be achievable.
  They need to be set out clearly so that they can be easily identified
  and understood. They need to be set out in such a way that it can
  be seen when they have been achieved.

- **It should include a time scale.**
  Usually a development plan will cover one year in detail and two
  further years in outline. Within the first year at least there should
  be clear indications of when activities are to happen and when
  targets are achieved. This way a school can 'pace' itself, making
  the best use of available time.

- **It should define responsibilities.**
  A development plan should specify not only what has to be done
  but also who is going to do it. It should define the responsibilities
  of individuals and teams. This way everybody knows what it is that
  is expected of them – and the headteacher knows what to expect.

- **It should outline resource and financial needs.**
  If activities are to take place and targets are to be achieved, then
  the necessary resources and finance must be made available. In
  defining a plan, a school must also examine and state the
  implications of putting it into operation. As schools become more
  accustomed to developmental planning and to financial delegation
  this aspect of a format should become more detailed and exact.

- **It should be presented as simply as possible.**
  The best plans are ones which encourage action. A complex
  format, while providing impressive documentation, can discourage
  action because it is inaccessible. Balance is important so that the
  plan can be seen to be a carefully constructed document, but also
  one which is useful on a day-to-day basis by those acting upon it.

The DES School Development Plans Project suggests a format of
four to five pages which might include

> - *the aims of the school*
> - *the proposed priorities and time scale*
> - *the justification of the priorities and their time scale*
> - *how the plan draws together different aspects of planning*
> - *the methods of reporting outcomes*
> - *the broad financial implications of the plan.*

Some schools have found it useful to have two development plans. The main plan is a professional and technical document which is available for reference in school – with perhaps three copies held in the school office, the staff room and the headteacher's room. Then there is a summary plan which is held by teachers and governors and is available for wider circulation if required.

Format 1

This format is a particularly simple one. It consists of a separate sheet for each area. These might be the six key areas advocated in this book or other areas identified by the school.

The main advantage of the format is its simplicity. It identifies needs and activities to meet those needs over a specified time scale, which includes not only the current year but also two further years. It can include reference to who is responsible for action and can also indicate financial priorities and INSET needs.

At the same time, however, its simplicity tends not to encourage detailed analysis. There is little space to include clear objectives and statements about evaluation. Nor is there much opportunity to include accurate costing.

It does have flexibility, though, and can be made to envelop these matters if a school wishes. It can also be regarded as a summary of the development plan, with more detailed information being recorded elsewhere.

A variation on this format is for a separate sheet to be used to show the responsibilities of each member of staff.

The formats presented here are actual examples of what has been devised and used in schools. It is most unlikely that you will find something which will suit your school perfectly. However, they might help you design your own.

SCHOOL DEVELOPMENT PLAN		
AREA		
NEED	ACTION	
	YEAR 1	YEARS 2 & 3

Format 2

This is a format with a "bias to action". It can be used with separate sheets for each defined area or for each member of staff. Alternatively it can be used as a continuous document with no specified divisions. It has columns indicating targets (what is to be done), actions to be taken (how it is to be done), time scales (by when), individual responsibilities (person responsible) and related issues (factors involved).

Again, this format has the advantage of simplicity. At the same time it can be used to include all the necessary information. By the use of columns it ensures that reference is made to responsibilities and time scales. By avoiding the use of the words target or objective, it may not be providing enough encouragement for precision. Similarly 'factors involved' is a broad heading and, by not being specified, detailed costing and INSET needs, for instance, might be omitted.

However, there is flexibility and scope to use the format to cover all requirements.

A school development plan can be at two levels. One approach is to have a central plan which is, in effect, a statement of the school's targets. This can then be supplemented by a more detailed action plan which deals in some detail with the activities planned to meet the targets.

School Self-Development

Sample Plan

What is to be done	How it is to be done	By when	Person Responsible	Factors Involved

Format 3

This is an individualised format. A sheet is prepared for each member of staff, setting out his or her objectives for the term (although this could be expanded to cover a full year). There is a space for ticks to indicate progress ('not started', 'current', 'achieved'. There is also a space for 'review and comments' – which could be completed by the member of staff or the headteacher (or the appraiser).

Its distinct advantage is that it enables a clear statement of what is expected of individuals within a given time scale. It also allows for monitoring of achievement.

Its major disadvantage is that, on its own, it does not provide a clear statement of the overall plan for the school. There is little opportunity to specify corporate objectives or to deal with finance and resources.

This format would relate to an appraisal programme with individual objectives which might extend beyond what is in the overall development plan. It might, in fact, be used to support a school development plan rather than to embody the plan itself.

TERMLY OBJECTIVES			
NAME: --			
TERM: FROM: TO:			
OBJECTIVES	Not started	Current	Achieved
Review and comments			

In 1851, John Ruskin wrote:

"In order that people may be happy in their work, these three things are needed: they must be fit for it; they must not do too much of it; and they must have a sense of success in it."

Format 4

This is a more complex format with a greater number of columns covering the various planning issues. It is an adaptation of a format used in secondary schools and can be used with a sheet for each term, or one for each area, or a combination of both.

It makes a distinction between general targets and more specific objectives. It also distinguishes between review and evaluation. The former is taken as meaning the way in which performance is monitored, and the latter as the way in which success will be judged. There are also spaces for indicating financial and in-service implications.

An advantage of this format is the level of detail it provides, covering a fairly wide range of the relevant issues. It can therefore be used to present a full picture of what is needed, what will be done to meet these needs, how the situation will be kept under review, and the implications of the planned activities.

In practice there might be too much information contained in too small a space, making the whole rather difficult to comprehend. There might also be limited flexibility – a column often prompts a response even when one is not appropriate.

Before adopting any particular format ask yourself the following questions:

- Is it simple?
  - flexible?
  - clear?
- Does it allow for a time scale
  - for individual responsibilities?
  - for resource and financial implications?
  - for INSET needs?
- Will it be clear when something has been achieved?
- Is it right for us?

SCHOOL DEVELOPMENT PLAN				Term.................	
Targets	Objectives	Design	Evaluate	Finance	Inset

Format 5

This format differs from the previous ones in that, while still being column-based, it approaches a matrix arrangement. It has spaces to indicate aims, objectives, methods, resources and cost. Again, separate sheets can be completed for each area and, where necessary, continuation sheets can be used.

Its major advantage is the emphasis it places on resources and cost while still maintaining a relative simplicity. It also creates a distinction between an overall aim and objectives to meet that aim. It distinguishes between those objectives and the ways in which they will be fulfilled. Such distinctions could be valuable in the quest for precision and clarity. Alternatively they could lead to space-filling without the addition of meaning.

A refinement of this format could involve a reversion to a purely column-based approach. The 'overall aim' could be placed at the top of the page and separate columns used for 'objectives' and 'method'.

SCHOOL DEVELOPMENT PLAN		
	Resources Needed	Cost
OVERALL AIM: OBJECTIVE 1 METHOD		
OBJECTIVE 2 METHOD		
OBJECTIVE 3 METHOD		

> "If we only have a vision, we are dreamers; if we merely work we are drudges. We need vision and work, hard work and clear vision."
>
> Dr Stanley Brown, quoted by Edward England in *An Unfading Vision*

Format 6

Another simple format but one with an added dimension – that of 'success criteria'. It allows for a statement of an overall aim for the area being considered. It then has columns for objectives and activities, and one for success criteria – the means by which achievement of the stated objectives will be judged.

Once again there is the benefit of simplicity and flexibility – although the effectiveness of the format depends on the way in which it is completed. There are no prompts for time scale, individual responsibility, in-service training, resources or finance, which could thus be excluded by default rather than by design. It does mean, however, that they can be included where appropriate but are not forced unnaturally by the existence of gaps.

On the other hand, success criteria are given a considerable prominence. They are highlighted as the way a school can gauge its own success. This prominence is significant as a reminder that evaluation of a development plan is an essential part of the whole process. It can lead to a 'tyranny of paper', however, as there may be occasions where achievement cannot be measured and formal success criteria are not appropriate. The very existence of a space in the format might tend to force an unrealistic response.

SCHOOL DEVELOPMENT PLAN
AIM

OBJECTIVES	ACTIVITIES	SUCCESS CRITERIA

"Targets must specify the criteria by which success in reaching a target can be judged at a later stage. These success criteria, which are a form of school-generated performance indicator, are the means for evaluating the plan, since they point to the evidence needed to judge successful implementation."

Hargreaves et al, Planning for School Development

Monitoring the Action 4

Why Should Action Be Monitored?

Thanks to Marshall McLuhan, one of the slogans of the 1960s was "the medium is the message". It became a hackneyed phrase but nevertheless carried a great deal of truth. It was a related truth which was conveyed in the older song lyrics: "It ain't what you do, it's the way that you do it. It ain't what you say, it's the way that you say it." It is just as applicable today – processes are as important as outcomes, and we need to look not only at results but also at the way those results were achieved.

That is not to say that we ignore the results. A football team which wins all its games but at the cost of fair play and attractive football is going to be pretty unpopular with everyone, apart from die-hard fans. At the same time, a team which plays marvellously but loses all its games might have a certain loyal following but is not going to progress very far. The ideal is a team that plays brilliantly and wins.

In terms of school development, we need to monitor both the extent to which our objectives are met and the way in which they are met. This is because the way in which they are met has an important influence on the eventual outcome. For the moment we will look at the latter – the 'action', or the processes of school development.

Monitoring the action is something which can take place annually or at the end of each development cycle. More usefully it should occur throughout the exercise. We need to be looking continually at what we are doing, how we are doing it, and whether we have chosen the best way to achieve our objectives.

If we take the audit stage, for example, we need to look at, for example:

- how we introduced the idea of school development
- how we identified what needed attention
- who was involved
- how they responded
- how the audit, itself, affected our organisation
- how it affected the children's education
- what documentation we used or generated
- how it was produced and circulated
- what meetings we held
- how they were organised.

Of course, we need to plan these things in advance, but by monitoring them while they are taking place – and after they have taken place – we can make sure that

- things are happening the way they should
- we are using effective procedures
- we are not hitting too many snags
- we do better next time.

We have heard a headteacher describe how he wrote the school development plan at home and then presented it to the staff as a finished document. We have also heard teachers complain at the number of extra meetings they have had to produce a school development plan. In both cases the effect of the plan is likely to be minimised by the medium of preparation. The objective was to produce a plan, but the process by which it was actually produced reduced its success.

Those cases might be extreme but they do show the importance of monitoring the action. By being aware of the implications of the actual process we can avoid the situation where we want a plan, get a plan, and then wonder why it doesn't work.

Some questions to ask

- Do the staff feel that they own the plan?
- Have we got the right time scales?
- Have we defined responsibilities?
- Is there something for everyone in the plan?
- Has anyone got too much to do?
- Has everyone got access to adequate professional support?
- Are the targets clearly stated?
- Will we know if we have been successful?
- How did we set about achieving this target?
- Why did we not achieve this target?
- Do we have the support of governors?
- Do we have the support of parents?
- What effect are we having on children's learning?

There are two things of which we can be certain:

> The processes don't just get right on their own.
> If the processes aren't right, then the plan won't be right.

In the DES booklet *The Management of Development Planning*, Hargreaves *et al* make it clear that

> *"Understanding school development planning seems to pass through three stages.*
>
> *1 A focus on the school development plan as an overall or comprehensive plan in the form of a document, which is probably supported by a range of other documents.*
>
> *2 A recognition that the process of school development planning, that is, the activities of constructing, implementing and evaluating a plan, are more important than the product, the plan as a document.*
>
> *3 A realisation that the management of planning is the key to successful development planning."*

Monitoring the action means monitoring the processes of development planning and its management.

The task of monitoring the action will almost certainly fall to headteachers, although in discharging it they can involve many other people, including colleagues on the staff, governors, parents and outsiders such as inspectors or consultants.

They can fulfil this task quite simply by talking – and listening. They need to talk to people about what is happening and listen very carefully and sensitively to what is said. (Although even this does not just happen. It needs an open atmosphere in which people feel secure.)

Some of the talking and listening can take place in formal settings – meetings and interviews. Although nobody wants more meetings at the moment, time set aside occasionally to discuss how things happen can be both productive and revealing. It can also be informal. Chats over coffee, passing remarks in a corridor, a periodic "How's it going?" – they can all contribute to the overall picture. And we must not forget that not only teachers have an interest and involvement. Non-teaching staff, governors, parents and children might all have their impressions of what is happening and of its effect – if we can only find the time to talk and to listen.

Once a school development plan has been drawn up and the implementation started using the established time scale, it is all too easy to leave things to take their own course, assuming that everything will happen as planned.

In fact things seldom, if ever, happen this way and it is essential to make comparisons between what we set out to achieve and what actually takes place. Evaluation is therefore a crucial part of the development process. The function of such evaluation is to keep a check on progress and also to provide information to help determine subsequent action.

There is a further danger – that evaluation is regarded as a separate and isolated stage in the development cycle, taking place when everything else has been done. It is in pointing out this danger that Hargreaves *et al* state that:

> *"...we treat the process of implementation and evaluation as interlaced, not as a period of implementation followed by a 'big bang' evaluation at the end."*

Even if the process of evaluation doesn't involve a 'big bang', some of the priorities and targets in your development plan will still be evaluated at the end of a cycle; others will need to be almost continuously evaluated.

The process by which you create your development plan will certainly need continual evaluation, as already discussed.

Checking on progress means finding out how things are going. It means checking the progress of targets that are probably still being worked on, rather than waiting until a particular time and then finding out whether everything has been finished. Different objectives and different activities involve different people and different time scales. Regular and systematic checks on progress make it possible to monitor the various different elements in order to ensure that progress is, in fact, being made and to make any necessary modifications to planned activities.

Who checks?

Checks on progress can be carried out by individuals or by groups. What is important is that the responsibility is identified. There are many possibilities.

The headteacher
- As the headteacher is ultimately responsible for ensuring that the school development plan is put into action, it might be best if he or she is also responsible for monitoring it. Yet by giving this responsibility to one person, it is possible to damage any sense of 'ownership' by the whole staff that may have been encouraged during the formulation of the plan. If this one person is the headteacher, then there is the added danger of alienation through a top-down model of evaluation.

A post-holder
- It is possible for the responsibility for checking on progress to be given to a particular individual – perhaps the deputy head or another 'senior' member of staff. Although there is still the possibility of restricting ownership of the plan, the danger is likely to be reduced by the fact that the designated person is not the headteacher.

A team
- Responsibility for checking on progress could be handed to a team of people instead of an individual. This team could already exist, for example, a management team consisting of the head, deputy and principal post-holders. Alternatively it could be a team established specifically for the purpose of monitoring the development plan. This has the advantage of involving more people and spreading the load. It creates extra work for some people, however, while still failing to involve everybody.

Everybody
- It is possible, and probably desirable, to involve everyone in the business of checking on progress. Individual members of staff, and any teams or working parties, can report on progress of the activities for which they are responsible. Such reports can be made to the headteacher or other designated person, to the management or monitoring team, and/or to the full staff. Where appropriate the person or group to which such reports are made can 'test' the accuracy of the report, and – again, if appropriate – the whole exercise can become a major part of any system of staff appraisal.

How often?

Checks on progress can happen almost continuously but it might be best for them to be timetabled so that they actually happen and do not get missed by default. One possibility is a dated series of meetings specifically for this purpose – individual appointments, team meetings, staff meetings and so on. These meetings could take place perhaps each term or each half term.

Another possibility is for regular interviews between individual staff and the headteacher or other designated person. Again, these interviews could take place termly or half-termly. Alternatively they could take place at times appropriate to the time scale relating to the individuals' own planned activities.

What does it involve?

Any checks on progress should involve various factors. These include:

- **Time scale**
  Was the activity completed on time? Will it be completed on time? If not, why not? Do we need a new time scale?
- **Success**
  Did/will the activity achieve the intended objective? If so, how? If not, why not? What could be/could have been done differently/ better?
- **The future**
  What needs to be done next? By the individual member of staff, by the team, by the school as a whole? Are there any short/long term implications to be drawn from what took place?

Some dangers

There are various dangers which can be involved in checking on progress.

Lack of time
Schools are busy places. Everyone in them is busy. Checking on progress is an addition to a growing list of activities. It may be regarded as essential – but so are very many other things which also require valuable time. The task of allocating time for checking on progress is one not only for the individual member of staff, but also for those who manage the school. It is necessary for heads, governors and LEAs to recognise that this activity, like so many others, must –

if it is to be carried out properly – receive an adequate allocation of resources, including the resource of time.

Lack of clarity

For the most part it is usually fairly easy to identify whether something has been done. What is not so easy is to identify its success. Sometimes an intuitive assessment can be made as to whether or not something went well but such intuition may be more in response to the ease of completion rather than to the effect on, say, the quality of children's learning. It is too easy to say "It was done", "It was good", or "The children enjoyed it", but such comments are not clear assessments of the success of an activity. Clarity in checking on progress can only take place when there was initial clarity of the objective to be met.

It isn't difficult to be clear about well-written 'instructional targets'. It is a lot harder to be clear about well-written 'expressive targets' (see Section 3.3).

Lack of purpose

With so many pressing tasks to be completed, school staff are unlikely to show commitment to something in which they can see little purpose. It appears to be a current fashion to ask teachers to complete evaluation sheets – about INSET sessions, publications, theatre performances, and so on. It can be a tedious exercise and the effect is not always apparent. If checking on progress is seen in the same light, it is not going to be taken seriously. It is essential, therefore, that there is a defined and honest purpose to the activity. This purpose should be more than checking up on whether people have carried out their duties. It should give full credit for success; it should involve learning from both achievement and non-achievement – taking into consideration those factors which cannot be controlled; and it should help to determine future objectives and future action.

Evaluating the achievement of objectives

There is no one single way of determining whether an objective has been achieved. Determination can be a very complex matter, although unsuccessful attempts are sometimes made to simplify it. It is too simplistic to think that success can always be measured. It is sometimes possible, but even then the difficulties experienced by those responsible for establishing reliable and usable performance indicators show how imperfect such an approach can be. It is also too simplistic to restrict any monitoring to checking whether or not an activity has taken place. Even when something has been done, there is no guarantee that it has achieved what has been intended.

A school needs to establish and adopt a whole range of processes of evaluation, using each one where and when appropriate. Many such processes have been listed by Graham Pountney in *Management in Action.*

Processes Of Evaluation

1 Formal testing
   • end of year examinations
   • standardised tests
   • weekly tests/quizzes.

2 Pupil profile
   • written by individual children
   • written periodically by teacher.

3 By observation of
   • children in the classroom
   • children around the school
   • lessons and class activities.

4 By talking to
   • individual teachers
   • various groupings of teachers
   • children
   • parents.

5 Progress records
   • kept by class or subject teacher.

6 By comparison with
   • other classes in the school
   • other schools
   • local or national statistics.

7 By seeking advice from
   • other colleagues
   • outside agencies
   • parents and the community.

8 By general impression of
   • classrooms
   • displays and exhibitions
   • teacher/child relationships
   • children's attitudes.

Each school will need to add to or extend this list as different methods of evaluation are devised. The most important task is to choose from the list the evaluational tool which will best suit the particular targets being evaluated.

A second audit

As well as checking on progress while implementation is still taking place, it is necessary to undertake an overall review of what has happened since the school development plan was initiated. In many ways this review is a second audit.

Timing
The review should take place at the end of a development cycle. In all probability this will be at the end of a school year. If the development plan covers a three-year period, it might be appropriate to conduct an annual mini-review with a major audit after three years.

Involvement
The review should, like the original planning process, involve as many people as possible. It will probably be co-ordinated by the headteacher or another senior member of staff, but this person should not conduct the review single-handed. The review should involve all those people whose work activities have been governed by the plan. It should also involve those whose lives have been affected by the activities. Finally it should include those who are responsible for the school's existence. Thus, the list of those to be active in the review might extend to teaching staff, non-teaching staff, children, parents, local community, governors and LEA officers. In reality, however, the review is likely to be undertaken by the teaching staff co-ordinated by the headteacher, referring to others where appropriate and possible.

Coverage
The progress checks which take place during the implementation of the plan tend to cover separate, sometimes quite small, elements of it in isolation from the rest. The review at, or towards, the end of the development cycle, however, covers the whole plan as a unit. The sort of questions to be asked are:

- to what extent did we achieve what we set out to achieve?
- how has the school changed since we started this round of development?
- how close are we to our original vision of what the school should be like?

The review process should, therefore, cover all those key areas identified by the school when it established its plan in the first place.

Conducting the review

Schools may work through the complete audit process again (see Sections 2.2 – 2.6). However, this is probably most useful at the end of a three-year cycle. At the end of each year of your development plan, a review might work like this.

Stage 1
The headteacher announces that the review is due to take place and gives the timetable for completion.

Stage 2
Each member of staff or each staff team reports to the headteacher on those elements of the plan for which they are responsible. The reports take into consideration:

- the original objectives
- planned activities
- unplanned activities
- measurable outcomes (using performance indicators as appropriate)
- non-measurable outcomes
- divergences from the original plan
- any known response from children, parents, inspectors, etc.

Such reports may be written or oral.

Stage 3
The headteacher checks reports by choosing certain elements and

- comparing his or her own information, understanding and perceptions with those of the reporting staff
- canvassing, or reviewing, the opinions and impressions of children, parents, inspectors, and so on
- scrutinising any performance indicators.

Stage 4
The headteacher collates the reports to produce one overall draft report.

Stage 5
The draft report is circulated to staff and then discussed at a staff meeting.

Stage 6
A final report is prepared and agreed. This report can then be used as
a report to the governing body and through them to parents –
although it is probable that a shorter, simplified version might be
better suited for this purpose.

What went wrong?

During the process of this review many achievements will be noted and
the report is an opportunity to celebrate success. Nevertheless, there will
quite certainly be aspects where things have not taken place as planned;
and probably some things which have resulted in failure. The review
should not ignore these but be taken as an opportunity to identify them
honestly (and usually openly) and to learn from what went wrong.

There are all sorts of reasons for things not proceeding as planned.

Staff absence or departure
The original school development plan will have identified tasks for
individual people. Members of staff are sometimes absent from
school for illness, maternity leave, jury service, and so on, preventing
them from carrying out the intended tasks. Other members of staff
leave tasks incomplete because of promotion, relocation, retirement,
infirmity, etc.

The best-managed organisations have plans to cope with staff
absences and departures. They operate shadow structures and
succession plans so that there is always someone to take over. Such
strategies are usually difficult to operate in primary schools, though.
Everyone has sufficient tasks and responsibilities of their own
without taking over someone else's. On top of that there is the
problem of recruitment which can leave vacancies unfilled or only
temporarily filled at a level which includes class teaching but no
additional responsibilities.

So, although there may be a skeleton of a plan to deal with staff
changes – particularly when they are not totally unexpected – each
situation has to be dealt with on its own merits. Decisions need to be
taken as to which activities are essential and which can be shelved,
and also as to who can be diverted from their own planned activities
to cover somebody else's. There is therefore a redefinition of
priorities and a reallocation of responsibilities.

Time

When plans are made, some implicit or explicit estimate is made concerning the amount of time required to fulfil what is required. Sometimes, happily, tasks take less time than expected. More often it seems – probably because of the very nature of people and tasks – they take considerably longer. The extra time might be because of

- an original miscalculation – in which case it is necessary to adjust time scales accordingly
- an overburdening of an individual or a team – in which case it is necessary to reallocate responsibilities
- a lack of personal organisation – in which case the individual needs additional guidance and/or support.

Unexpected occurrences

One of the advantages of school development plans is the way in which they reduce the unexpected. By planning in advance, things come as less as a surprise. Yet it is still not possible to predict confidently everything that will happen. When the unexpected happens, it then becomes necessary to think again about priorities, and if extra work needs to be done, schools must decide what is to be dropped or delayed.

- Faced with a local controversy about reading methods and standards a school decided to examine its own policies, delaying the planned emphasis on children's writing to a later date.
- Losing its roof and a great deal of equipment in a storm, a school had to reconsider its entire physical organisation. This led to an unplanned concentration on the school environment in place of other, planned activities.
- The local inspectorate announced a systematic review of its schools; the timing of the extended visit and of the required documentation cut across other planned activities which were modified or delayed.
- The delay in production of National Curriculum history and geography reports, and uncertainty about their likely contents, resulted in a postponement of a planned review of teaching through topic work.

Self-management

Sometimes objectives are not fulfilled, tasks not completed, and deadlines not met because of what can best be described as 'poor management'. This might, for instance, involve inefficient use of a diary, poor time management, or personal inefficiency. The underlying reasons might be difficult to identify, as might the remedy Some form of in-service training might be helpful but there might also be a need for individual direction and guidance. Finally, and regrettably, disciplinary action might be required.

There is another way in which your development plan might be reviewed – through the official review of the school conducted by your LEA. We discuss the important links between school development plans and formal reviews in Section 5.6.

School development planning is about a systematic approach to organising a school. If this approach is documented, it follows that the results should also be documented – otherwise it is like a book with some of the chapters missing.

Audience

It is necessary to report on the outcomes of school development for a variety of people with a need – or a right – to know what is happening.

Headteachers will probably have the responsibility of compiling any reports on outcomes. In addition they need such reports for their own purposes. Headteachers must monitor progress with the development plan. This requires the gathering and interpretation of information. They will obtain some of the information by their own means and will also receive reports – written and oral – from others. They might try to retain such information by memory but it would be more appropriate to record it in written form. Headteachers can thus keep a check on progress and also be in a position to make or guide decisions on future action.

The **staff** also have two separate but complementary roles on reporting on outcomes. They need to report on their own activities – probably to the headteacher but perhaps also to other individual staff (such as team leaders) and to the staff as a whole. They do this to provide information and also to report progress on their individual targets. They also need to receive reports so that they are informed on what is happening and so that they can make decisions relating to their own activities. It shouldn't be forgotten that staff also need to know the outcomes of the development plan so that they can celebrate the success of their own work. Without celebration, school development planning runs the risk of becoming another mechanistic and dull exercise.

The **governors** need to receive reports on outcomes so that they can fulfil their own responsibilities relating to overseeing the way in which the school is operating. Having agreed the school development plan in the first place, they will want to know about the progress made with the action it initiated. They will probably also need such reports so that they can fulfil any obligations they have to report to central government, the local authority and parents.

The **LEA** needs to receive reports so that it can meet its own obligations. These include the duty to monitor the educational provision in individual schools. By reporting to the LEA on the outcomes of a development plan, a school is providing it with valuable evidence about what is actually happening. An LEA also has a duty to ensure that it is providing an effective service throughout its area. Again, it can obtain valuable evidence for this on the basis of the reports received from each establishment.

The **parents** (and potential parents) of a school might be considered as having a right to access to reports on the outcomes of the development plan. The contents of such reports can help them to make informed decisions about their children's education. Providing this information helps a school to meet its duties of accountability.

Contents

The contents of a report on the outcomes of a school development plan could or should include reference to two major aspects:

• **The process**
  This involves information about how the plan was devised and how it was monitored. It also includes factors which might have affected the original plan and also its implementations. Details can be given of any changes to the original plan and the reasons for such changes.

• **The results**
  At its simplest this can involve 'ticking off' aims and individual objectives as they are achieved or completed. It can also include a commentary on the achievement of these aims and objectives. Where appropriate, reference can be made to any success criteria or relevant performance indicators.

The report might also contain other information in an appendix. Such information might cover factual and statistical details relating to, for instance, staffing, school roll, test scores and finance.

Frequency

The frequency of reporting the outcomes of a school development plan is dependent upon the audience and the purposes of such reports.

For a headteacher and staff the report needs to be continuous. They need to be monitoring progress continually and therefore need to receive reports from staff at appropriate intervals related to the implementation timetable. They will also occasionally need to report informally to governors and inspectors at short notice and therefore must have information easily available in a suitable form.

Governing bodies meet at least termly and receive reports from the headteacher on the conduct of the school. Although they are unlikely to require a full school development plan report on each occasion, they might consider that they need an interim report each term. In any event, the headteacher's general report will almost certainly always include some reference to progress with the plan.

Parents receive an annual report from the governors. Although this report might not include detailed information about the development plan, it might be considered an appropriate interval for the governors to receive a report on outcomes so that they are properly informed and can pass on any relevant details. The LEA might also require an annual report, which might be linked with a systematic review of the school by the inspectorate.

As three years is often regarded as a suitable period for the development cycle, it is also possible that governors and/or LEAs might also require a triennial report.

Formats

The format of a report on outcomes will depend on the audience. It will also depend on the format of the original version of the development plan received by each audience.

The headteacher and other members of the school teaching staff (and possibly some of the non-teaching staff) will each have a full version of the plan – including details of individual targets – and will therefore need a full version of any report.

The governing body, except the chairperson, might have received a summarised version of the plan. This might have included the overall aims and general objectives without the individual targets. In this case they will require a report which relates to what they have received. The same might apply to the LEA.

Parents and others have access to all non-confidential papers received by a governing body – and this will include a development plan and any reports on outcomes. They might also have received a résumé of the plan – possibly as part of the governors' annual report – and should then receive a résumé of any report on outcomes.

By reporting on the outcomes of a school development plan, a school is able to show that it is monitoring the implementation of the plan. It is also able to provide, to those who require it, proof that appropriate action is being taken to develop the school and thus improve the education it provides.

The development cycle

School development is a continuous cycle. There are no times when development is not taking place and few times when progress is not being checked. Thus, any review of performance and achievement has to take place within the context of continued implementation. It is rather like a photographic snapshot, appearing to freeze action for a brief, unique instant. The action is not, in fact, halted, and when the image is viewed the moment has passed and things have already changed.

There are a number of reasons for conducting a review.

Looking back
It is useful, and generally rewarding, to look back on what has been done and what has been achieved. Achievement can be celebrated and it is often surprising and encouraging to see what has been done. At the same time it is instructive to see what has not been done.

Evaluation
Actions are taken to fulfil certain stated objectives. A review is a chance to evaluate the validity of those original objectives. It is also a chance to evaluate the extent to which the actions taken served to fulfil the objectives.

Audit
The school development cycle generally starts with an audit – an analysis of the school, asking the question "Where are we now?" A review deals with the same question, although not always in the same depth. Future full audits, perhaps every three years, will incorporate a review of development.

Future action
By examining what has gone before, a review provides information about what needs to be done in the future. In a three year rolling plan some objectives and activities will already be sketched out. Other things – planned but not completed – must, if they are still valid, be carried forward into the new cycle. Finally, action taken over one period frequently leads to an identification of actions which need to be taken in a subsequent period.

When planning for the next cycle of development, various factors need to be taken into consideration. These include:

- Long term plans already identified. Perhaps actions planned for the second and third years of a three year cycle. Do they still apply? Are they still needed?
- Actions not yet taken. Perhaps we changed our priorities or just ran out of time. Are they still relevant? Have they been taken over by other events? Will they really be done this time round?
- Changes of staff. Changes of staff can lead to changes of direction. Are there any new perceptions? Are there strengths on which to build? Are there weaknesses to overcome? Changing staffing levels are also significant, and existing staff frequently develop new expertise which can be put to good use.
- New contexts. Schools do not exist in isolation from the wider contexts. Are there any government initiatives requiring a response? Any local initiatives? Any new perceptions among governors or parents that need to be considered?
- Changing circumstances. A school's immediate physical circumstances can change with considerable effect on the school. A rebuilding programme, a new housing development, a new main road are all examples of major changes which demand a response.

It is not generally convenient or an efficient use of time and resources to carry out a full-scale audit of a school each year. Nevertheless, a careful and systematic review of planned development can be used to assess what has gone before and to make further detailed plans for the future. Without such a review it is not possible to judge the effectiveness of what has taken place, or even if the the appropriate objectives were set and the appropriate activities planned in the first place. Nor is it possible to make informed decisions about what remains to be done.

Background Issues   5

Delegation is one of those concepts which is frequently applauded, often set down in documentation and just as often not acted upon.

In *The Managerial Work of Primary School Headteachers* Alan Coulson recognises a certain type of head who sees himself as a charismatic knight riding around 'his' school slaying dragons and saving maidens – Coulson doesn't mention who is clearing up after the horse! This view of the headteacher as a powerful leader and decision maker, always centre stage, is inappropriate for the 1990s – and impossible for the headteacher to fulfil. School development plans need delegation – they cannot be achieved by one person alone.

For schools to survive and prosper in the foreseeable future, delegation is not only desirable but essential.

Power and responsibility

Two key concepts associated with delegation are power and responsibility. Power and the desire to keep it is what frequently stops genuine delegation. Many people will hide under a defensive cloak with such statements as "Most of my staff are too inexperienced ; it's too risky," or "I like to be busy and work best under pressure, so why bother to delegate?" or "I'm just protecting my staff – they have too much to do already."

Real delegation must involve the transference of power. Responsibility is a different matter. Ultimately, responsibility must remain in the hands of the person doing the delegating; it is up to them to check that the delegated power is being used effectively.

At a day-to-day level the responsibility is often shared or even taken by the person to whom the authority has been delegated. In most staffrooms, if Fred makes a mess of organising the staff rotas everyone knows who's responsible! Nevertheless, the final responsibility isn't Fred's. He has been delegated the power to do something – but not the final responsibility for it.

> *"Under LMS the headteacher, after consultation, decided to delegate responsibility for monitoring and allocating funds for supply teachers to a small sub-committee of three teachers. They reported to the head on how this part of the budget was going every month and made decisions about insurance, who to bring in etc.*

> *At the end of the Autumn Term the budget was over half spent because of an outbreak of 'flu and the resulting high number of absences. Over Christmas the head worried about this and at the start of the Spring Term called the sub-committee in to his office and said he'd decided that they would all have to 'cover' the first two days of any absence in order to protect the budget."*

Who was given the power? Who took the responsibility? A few years ago, ultimate responsibility was fairly clearly with the headteacher, but the Education Reform Act has changed all that. It is clear that in this situation the ultimate responsibility would be with the governors. So why are three teachers trying to run the supply budget? Well, the governors have delegated this task to the headteacher who has then delegated it to the staff! The problem here was that the head had not really let go of his power. Real delegation requires you to

- let go
- trust someone
- and still be responsible.

It's not an easy thing to do.

Equally, delegators cannot just turn their backs on what's happening. The trust given to the delegatee should be built on a knowledge of the experience, judgement and capability of that person or group of people. In this way the people delegating have some confidence that the job will be done reasonably well and often better than they might do it themselves. *Control* however is not lost by the delegator – they should retain control but exercise it with caution and care.

Delegation is often a two-way process. Most of us will have seen how power can change people – often for the worse. The supportive deputy with a full-time teaching commitment can become the autocratic, non-supportive headteacher almost overnight. This has a lot to do with the powerful position of the head in the British educational system, and with the frequently impossible demands made upon the head which can generate a sense of loneliness and frustration. If we consider some of the areas where the head has potentially great power we can begin to see how vital it is for the development of effective schools that delegation be taken seriously.

The headteacher has the power to

- control communication systems – eg sifting the mail
- take executive decisions – eg assemblies will be at 3 pm instead of 9.10 am
- control meetings – eg closing down debate from the chair
- approve or disapprove – eg thanking or not thanking staff who have run a residential trip
- affect careers – eg by telephoning unattributable information to another head
- affect the image of the school – eg by the way letters are written to parents.

The implications of all this are to ensure that delegation has an agreed framework where

- jobs are matched to people's abilities
- tasks are negotiated and clearly defined
- resource implications are taken on board
- ownership of the tasks is clearly with the delegatee
- delegation is seen as contributing towards building collaboration
- everyone knows what has been delegated and to whom.

Accountability

Clearly there is an accountability factor inherent in most delegation. Before things go wrong this needs to be understood by everyone. Whatever actions take place and whatever judgements are made about those actions, there should be some sort of rationale which can be seen to be operating. Such an approach makes reporting back on decisions and so on much easier. It's worth bearing in mind that there will be an obligation to let people know what's happening so that all the staff can be aware and, if appropriate, have their say. This is important as there is a danger in a 'cosy' relationship building up between head and delegatee which can cause resentment.

How should you delegate?

- Make sure the roles and responsibilities are clear.
- Define any time scales that might be involved.
- Provide any necessary materials, information, support.
- Explain how the delegated role fits into the overall plans for the school.

- Arrange for mutually agreed progress reports if appropriate.
- Decide on an agreed method of evaluation.
- Praise and encourage whenever possible.

School development plans and delegation
Effective delegation is inextricably linked with the success of school development planning. The process of producing a plan and the execution of the targets identified within the plan will require many headteachers to delegate at least

- the running of meetings
- the production of reports and papers
- contact with various members of the school constituency
- financial spending
- interpersonal contact between colleagues.

To delegate such matters ineffectively is to harm the process of development planning; to delegate effectively is to encourage its success.

The importance of collaborative work

People charged with the running of primary schools have a large number of responsibilities ranging from health and safety to implementing the National Curriculum, from developing social, intellectual and emotional aims for their pupils to maintaining a clean and attractive environment. Often this has to be done in a climate that is neither economically nor socially supportive. It is not a task that can be successfully undertaken by an individual – Sir Keith Joseph's view of the headteacher as "the nearest thing we have to a magic wand" is not appropriate. It requires **collaboration** between staff and, eventually, all those who work with the school in trying to realise its aims.

Collaboration between groups
For example, if a school decides to produce a multicultural policy document the following groups might (and perhaps should) be involved:

- all teachers
- teacher's support staff
- part-time staff
- governors
- parental representatives
- the advisory service
- local community leaders.

Of course, not all of these groups will meet together and not all of them will, necessarily, take part in person – some may be consulted and use written material to have an input. But the collaboration is a vital part of the process.

Perspectives
If we think about producing such a multicultural policy, each group involved will have its own perspectives on any given issue. The sub-group of staff (which may include ancillary staff) will probably be committed to the concept, the members of the PTA may, as a group, be unclear as to the purpose of the policy and may even be antagonistic. There could well be a group of teachers who share the view that this is a peripheral issue for them.

Just as there are group perspectives, so there are individual perspectives. The multicultural adviser will bring a wide experience and understanding of local ethnic groups and be aware of the problems which may be inherent among staff working in the school. The governor may bring a political viewpoint and may have very limited experience of the issue involved. A teacher may see the whole thing as irrelevant and a left-wing plot!

Awareness and understanding

To gain some sort of genuine collaboration between groups and individuals must involve an approach which is concerned with reducing conflict and increasing mutual respect wherever possible.

This requires an ability to understand others, their concerns, perspectives, motives and roles. Remember, we are talking about all those individuals, groups and organisations which impinge on the school context from outside, as well as the broad grouping who make up the staff (in its widest sense) and work inside the school. We have previously described this as 'the school constituency', identifying seven groupings as having some effect on how the school functions.

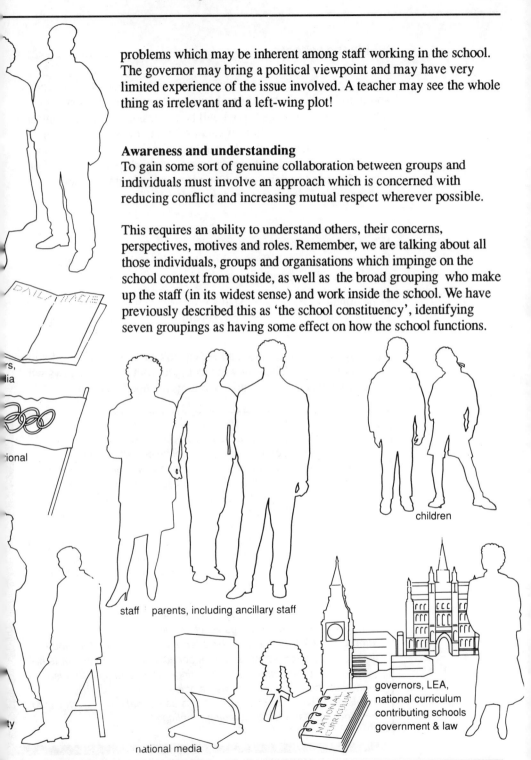

children

staff   parents, including ancillary staff

national media

governors, LEA, national curriculum contributing schools government & law

Within the school

For some teachers, their level of contact with certain outside groups and individuals will be minimal, and for most the day-to-day working relationships within the school will be of most importance. Central to the concept of the collaborative school and to the success of school development plans is an understanding of others. Some people have a natural empathy and willingness to see another's point of view but most of us need to develop such understandings and to work at making them more than a grudging tolerance.

What does this mean in practice?

It requires us to use different skills and approaches for different people – it will depend upon such things as

- personality
- motivation
- status
- self-esteem
- experience
- opportunities.

Apart from the first of these, all are capable of being developed within the school context. The following example from a school shows what can easily happen if such understandings are not displayed.

"Mike was efficient, punctual, a bit pompous and well-organised. He had been a PE teacher in a prep school before moving to his present job as a class teacher with responsibility for mathematics. His interests were sporting and he went for a daily run at lunch times except for one day when he ran a badminton club. He often worked late into the evening.

Lisa had trained as a designer specialising in textiles and although a bit chaotic sometimes, she ran a happy and successful class. She usually arrived in school about 7.45, worked during the lunch hour and left soon after school finished.

Both teachers were highly regarded by the parents. The head arranged a series of meetings which required Lisa and Mike to attend. The meetings were to be over a five week period at lunch times. Mike protested and said that because of his commitments he would much prefer after school meetings. The head agreed. Lisa found out, stormed in to the head's office and asked for the meetings to be put back to lunch times as her pattern of work would be seriously disrupted by evening meetings."

All three participants in this episode lacked understanding of each other which would have helped resolve this conflict.

How might this be achieved?

First, by being aware of **individual perspectives**. Lisa and Mike had different educational experiences, different work patterns, different attitudes and so on, but they also had things in common – commitment, professionalism and so on. To get the best from them and for them, the head needed to understand this. The most effective management decisions will invariably have a knowledge of individual perspectives as part of the decision making process.

Second, by **management planning**. If a new series of meetings is sprung upon anyone, including those demanded of the head by the LEA or governors, then problems are likely to be encountered. School development plans can help overcome this by setting out timetables that will have, hopefully, sorted out the competing personal claims long before the meetings start.

Third, by **knowing what people think**. Perhaps we should add to this 'and trying to appreciate their situation'. If Lisa had realised how important Mike's running was to him, and he had realised how important getting home soon after school was to Lisa, there could have been some room for compromise. If we know how strongly people feel about something we can often take action that will help mutual understanding.

Outside the school

Although it is relationships within the school that are the most crucial element in affecting children's learning, headteachers and, increasingly, other teachers have a host of links with groups and individuals from outside the school.

parents   medical practitioners   councillors

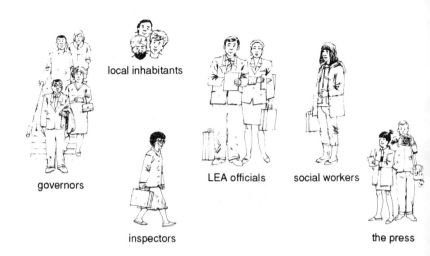

Understanding their perspectives is vital. Mistakes in dealing with the media, for example, can be very damaging, and sometimes unavoidable! But there is less chance of this happening if we come to a shared understanding with some of these groups, realising their concerns, priorities and perspectives. Accepting differences as inevitable and trying to deal rationally with them gives authority to your actions and support to your school.

Understanding others is one of the key tasks of management. In his book *13 Fatal Errors Committed by Managers and How to Avoid Them*, W Steven Brown states

> "A manager who tries to direct each member of his staff in the same way, using a single technique, can expect to be greatly let down ... An effective manager is aware of the differences in personality of his staff, and taking their strengths and weaknesses into account, directs them by above all treating them as individuals."

Such an approach lies at the heart of understanding others.

School development planning demands organisation. By its very nature a school development plan is an organisational tool. The school which is disorganised will find it much harder to produce an effective development plan. We only have to think of the many functions a school has to carry out to see that this is so:

- **Meetings** – staff, senior management, curriculum, teams, groups, etc.
- **Communication systems** – letters to parents, handing out information, exchanging pupil-based records, governors' reports, etc.
- **Administrative procedures** – ordering and paying for stock and equipment, dealing with school dinners, producing reports and teaching materials, controlling the staff salary budget, etc.
- **Class management** – allocating pupils to classes, allocating teachers to classes, deciding on use of space, deciding on furniture and fittings, etc.
- **Outside agencies** – working with health authorities, educational psychologists, social services departments, educational welfare officers, police, private and LEA contractors, etc.

Even this brief overview makes it clear that a disorganised school will find itself with serious difficulties.

Hidden messages

The organisation of your school conveys important hidden messages, too.

A new governor was being shown round a large primary school. She worked as a pharmacist and had not been in a school for many years, not having children of her own. The headteacher had sent her various documents prior to the visit – a staff handbook, curriculum statements, and so on – and was now explaining some of the background organisation which underpinned the smooth running of the school. On returning to the head's office the governor slumped exhausted into a chair as the head excused herself to momentarily deal with a sick child. When the two finally resumed their conversation the governor said, "I don't think I've understood a half of it – but I'm very impressed with the way everything runs."

Schools are very complex places and their effectiveness demands a high level of managerial skill; it also demands that they be well organised. There is a feeling among some teachers that 'organisation' is a pejorative word, conjuring up images of bureaucracy, regimentation and lack of freedom. There is a common notion that by instinct many teachers are creative, people-orientated and not given to being 'organised'. We need to knock that argument on the head. Of course, a school can be over-organised so that freedom to respond to children's needs and to unforeseen circumstances is restricted, but on the whole the teachers who have any real sense of professionalism and care for their pupils will despair at the disorganised school. Go into any school and you will very soon pick up on the type of organisation you've entered.

Where's the evidence of organisation?

Here are some items which a visitor (and it will depend on what sort of visitor – parent, inspector, officer, etc) might well encounter and which will, without reference to written or verbal statements, tell them about the school's organisation.

How is the visitor greeted?

- Do they have to wait in an entrance area hoping someone will appear?
- Are they treated courteously by a member of the support staff?
- Do teachers and/or other adults rush past and ignore them?
- Do they have a place to sit and wait?
- If they're there for an appointment, does the secretary know their name?
- Are they expected?

What are the displays like?

- Do they reflect a range of work from across the curriculum?
- Do they represent work from different age-groups?
- Are they well presented?
- Are they changed at appropriate times?
- Are the school's and individual's achievements on show?
- Is some of the work three dimensional?
- Are some of the displays interactive?

How do people move around the building?

- At the end of break, is there corridor chaos?
- Are there children wandering around aimlessly during lessons?
- Is there adequate supervision when major movements take place?
- How do children leave the room at the end of a session?
- How do children enter a room at the start of a lesson?
- Are the staff apparently in the right place at the right time?

How accessible are the school's resources?

- Is there a well-stocked and organised library?
- Are resources available to children?
- Are basic materials easily accessed by staff?
- Are some classrooms better stocked and resourced than others?
- Are scarce resources (perhaps computers) shared equitably?

The cartoon is based upon a real incident. So often the organisation, at its most basic level, affects the relationships and ethos of the school. The way human beings react to their working environment, the way they organise its resources, its communications systems, its physical space and so on has a profound effect on what happens in that place.

Schools need to exhibit an organised context not as some spurious image-making device but as a true reflection of their values and aims.

Organisation and school development plans

Handy and Aitken helped define the background to school development plans long before we called them by that name.

> "What is important is that the organisation knows its way – where it is going – and that those working in the organisation know what it stands for and what are the shared set of values to which each is contributing ... The definition of roles and responsibilities and the choosing of staff to undertake them is a crucial task for any head, and it can present difficulties."

We were reminded of this when listening to an adviser telling us of a visit she had made to a school which was having difficulties sorting out its approach to the National Curriculum. On entering the headteacher's office she was faced with two desks, one for the head and one for his secretary, and a scene of near chaos. Papers and files were stacked everywhere and there was no apparent system for storing and retrieving information. As she soon discovered, the office reflected the general malaise that existed throughout the school. It was hardly surprising that the school was having difficulty in organising its development plan – it existed in a completely disorganised context.

So the systems, class structure, use of offices, classrooms, other spaces, the definitions of responsibilities, the rules and codes of conduct, the implementation of LMS and so on and so on all contribute to an organisational structure that can enhance or debilitate the work that goes on in the school. It is the organisation elsewhere that creates the climate within which school development plans can proceed.

The Open University course The Effective Manager begins a section called 'Managing your time' with the words

> "Next, let us examine very briefly some ideas for handling what for many managers is their most intractable and stressful problem, shortage of time."

Increasingly, everyone is having to face up to the problem of not having enough time. In every business where demands are placed upon managers the problem of finding available time is evident.

One of the difficulties is that there cannot be any more time than there is – there can't be more than 24 hours in a day or seven days in a week. Another is that there seem to be some people who are capable of doing more, of being more organised, than others. It isn't as though those people have found more time – what they are able to do is to manage the time they have more effectively.

Managing a classroom or a school is a complex and time-consuming process. School development plans can help that process but they, too, need managing. Our ability to use the time we have most productively will exert a critical influence on the way we are able to achieve our targets.

This and the next two sections provide some ideas which might enable you to think about how you can manage your own personal time and that of your organisation.

Personality counts

Our personality has an effect upon our ability to manage the time we have available. In his book *The Complete Time Management System*, Christian Godefroy suggests three characteristics which interfere with effective time management.

First, you may be a perfectionist. If you are, you

- are likely to be worried about what other people think of you
- may put off doing things in case you fail
- may work endlessly at something, always trying to improve it that little bit more

- always think you could have done something better
- may take a long time to do either simple or relatively unimportant things.

Being a perfectionist uses up endless amounts of time. Winston Churchill was once asked by someone how to spell perfection. The answer he gave was p-a-r-a-l-y-s-i-s. Not being a perfectionist does not mean being slapdash – there is a middle ground, which involves doing things as well as possible in the time available.

Second, you may be a *workaholic*. If you are, you

- love working very hard
- set goals which you often fail to reach
- can't stand being inactive
- feel guilty if you relax or slow down
- prefer doing to reflecting
- accept more work than you can handle
- have difficulty balancing your personal and professional life
- are often stressed.

Workaholics get a lot of things done. The question is, do they get them done well and do they get them done with the co-operation of others?

Third, you may be in almost permanent *crisis*. If you are, you

- feel you have little control over outside events
- are unlikely to plan well – including ignoring warning signals, overloading your schedule, not planning far enough ahead
- may be poor at estimating deadlines
- enjoy the feeling of pressure
- find it hard to face up to the facts of a situation.

Crises are the enemy of effective working.

There are other personal characteristics which affect the ability to manage time well. The point is to realise that the problem is not always external – it may be connected with who we are. If you recognise yourself as any of the three types mentioned above it is worth spending a few minutes considering the effect it has had upon your effectiveness in your job.

Remedying the situation isn't always easy. You may have spent years practising to be a perfectionist, a workaholic or a crisis lover! But if you recognise your own characteristics as part of your time management problem, you have to begin to accept the need to begin the process of change. As a contribution towards beginning the change, you might

- think about whether wanting to be absolutely right is really most beneficial for you or your organisation – and whether it is realistic?
- stop doing anything for a while – except work out what your genuine priorities are
- try and ensure that you volunteer for involvement where your strengths will be an asset and not a hindrance
- think about the effects on others of your non-stop approach to your life and work.

You may do any number of things which enable you to face up to the part your personality plays in the management of your own time. You might even be surprised at what you discover.

Personal organisation

It may take a while both to understand how personality affects ability to manage time and to respond to that understanding. But, the way we organise ourselves can also contribute to the release of more time. There are steps we can take which can help us to be more effective. Here are just some points to think about.

1 Are your personal priorities sorted out?
School development plans are about making priorities for the school – in one sense, development planning is a school-based time-management exercise. But we need to make sure we have gone through a similar process ourselves. Faced with a mass of personal and professional demands, the only way we have of knowing which to give time to and which to leave alone is to judge each of them against our own personal set of priorities.

We need to think about our personal and professional lives; the responsibilities we have in both. Try these exercises.

- Decide whether you are going to think about your personal or professional life.
- Write down as quickly as possible everything you have to do connected with that area of your life. Try not to leave anything out.
- Leave the list alone for ten minutes and then return to it. Is there anything you want to add?
- Divide another piece of paper into three columns, headed 'A', 'B', and 'C'.

- In the 'A' column write down the things it is absolutely vital for you to do.
- In the 'B' column write down the things that you should do.
- In the 'C' column write down the things you could do.

Keep this piece of paper close by you. As much as possible, make sure that you do something towards an 'A' activity each day; try and achieve an 'A' activity as soon as you can. Reward yourself when you manage it. Every so often, choose a 'B' activity. Occasionally, deal with a number of 'C' activities together.

The saying "The immediate takes precedence over the important" is proved true time and time again because we haven't worked out what the really important is. Use as much of the time you have to deal with what really matters to you.

2 How much time do you waste?
For many of us this question often promotes indignation when it is first asked – but just look at the number of ways in which it is possible to waste time:

- Don't establish priorities.
- Try hard not to be informed.
- Don't have a daily agenda.
- Don't say "No".
- Spend too long over coffee in the staffroom.
- Enjoy meetings.
- Communicate badly.
- Allow too many interruptions.
- Spend too long on the telephone.

Think of your own additions to this list . If you dare, ask a good friend or close colleague to help you identify your own time wasters.

Work out how much time you waste. (Do you realise, for example, that if a teacher take five minutes longer than a colleague to settle a class back to work after assembly, morning, lunchtime and afternoon breaks then, over a year, that colleague's children will have worked an extra 63 hours, or three working weeks, longer?).

Choose some of the time wasters and begin to deal with them. It is possible to achieve some time savings very quickly. (Do you really need to have a conversation with every colleague down the corridor?)

3 How is your reading?

Every teacher and headteacher rightly comments about the amount of reading matter which comes into school – it is overwhelming. It seems unlikely to change, however, and so the most important question is, how can we read what has to be read most efficiently?

What kinds of reading skills do you possess? For example:

- Are you easily distracted when you read?
- Do you read everything in the same way?
- Do you always read at the same speed?
- Can you grasp the overall concept of an article or document easily?
- Do you skim before you read?

All of these will have an effect upon the quality of your reading. They affect the time it takes you to read documents but they also affect the amount of time you spend in other ways. Reading a document ineffectively means that you waste time by not passing on information accurately, by having to re-read it, by failing to take advantage of opportunities those documents contain or by responding to them inappropriately.

The good news is that almost everyone can be helped to improve their reading skills and reading speed. With the amount of documentation arriving in schools it could be one of the best savers of time you have ever found.

There are plenty of other ways in which you can improve your personal use of time – including working to your internal clock or making use of dead time, such as waiting to pick up your children, or time spent travelling on a train. Perhaps one of the most effective is to identify a colleague who seems to be able to do so much more than you and study them. Observation of others can teach so much.

Section 5.3 dealt with 'the organised school' . It stressed the need for an effective organisation if school development planning is to take place effectively; equally, it stressed that the organisation of the school creates a good or bad climate.

The way in which the school is organised can also save or lose a tremendous amount of time. Just consider some of the following situations.

1 In the office

- Have you an area in which meetings with parents or colleagues can be held without interruption?
- Does the filing system enable information to be retrieved easily (within two minutes) or with difficulty?
- Is the filing system cluttered with out-of-date material?
- Is the office equipped to cope with the demands placed on it – could the school make use of an answerphone? Do you handwrite your letters and give them to a secretary to re-type or do you use a dictating machine? Do you have a wordprocessor or a manual typewriter?
- Does the desk space you have help or hinder the amount of time it takes you to perform tasks?
- Is the office cluttered with jumble, lost property and so on? (Is there really nowhere else it can go?)

2 In the resource areas

- Is everything clearly labelled?
- Is the storage equipment a help or a hindrance to easy access?
- How much of the equipment is out of date?
- How much of the equipment has been unused for the past two years?

3 Around the school

- Are the systems appropriate for the effective and efficient movement of children?
- Is information distributed in the most effective way? (Is a book sent round during lesson time the most effective way of using time and space?)
- Are your meetings run effectively? (See Section 5.5.)
- Is everyone aware of what they are supposed to be doing? (See Section 3.6.)

Today

Wednesday 15th November

9.15   Doctor in

11.00   Governor visiting

1.15   Head out

It helps to invite a friend or a sympathetic outsider to consider these questions with you. So many of the things we do in school are done only because a tradition has grown up that this is how it should be – but it doesn't have to be that way. If we can begin to be aware of the amount of time our present systems are using we can begin to make decisions about the changes required. In most cases, decisions are more effective than traditions.

This section on time management has only given a flavour of the opportunities there are to create more usable time from that which we have available. We hope it might have enabled you to identify one or two areas in which more time can be gained, but we hope you will look at the subject in more detail. We all need to make the best use of the time we have.

School development plans are not 'headteacher development plans' or 'small group of teachers development plans'. They are whole-school plans, which means that the widest possible consultation should take place as part of their production process. However, this does not mean that a whole series of full staff meetings with governors, ancillary and support staff, advisers/inspectors and parents is the most effective way of achieving this. In relationship to school development plans, well run meetings can provide three crucial elements:

1 a commitment to decisions
2 ownership of the plan
3 motivation to carry it out.

Meetings are an integral part of school development planning and, as such, the basic ground rules are worth reiterating.

Purpose
Whatever happens once the meeting is under way, its purpose must be clear – not only to you but to those attending. The purposes of the meetings may be

- to inform
- to consult
- to recommend action

- to make decisions
- to discuss issues
- to have a good time.

Who comes to the meeting?
If you are meeting to discuss elements of the curriculum to be focused on during the next year you won't need the caretaker along and, equally, if you're looking at ways of improving the appearance of the school, you will. So who needs to be there should be clear, as well as considering who might like to be invited. One useful device to keep meetings small is to have an open invitation, with the proviso that those who are not actually members of that particular group or committee can only contribute at the discretion of the chairperson.

Where and when will the meeting be held?
This seems so self-evident that you might think it not worth mentioning, but the bigger the school and the greater the number of meetings, the more important this becomes. Giving good notice, preferably having a regular time slot, is very important to people with complicated lives and a host of commitments. The location of the meeting is important too – adults and small chairs don't mix well! Yet there are still some primary schools where there aren't enough comfortable chairs to go round.

Are any special equipment or materials needed?

There is nothing worse than arriving at a meeting only to be asked for last year's topic plans, exam results or whatever, which of course you haven't brought. The meeting gets delayed and the person concerned can be embarrassed/annoyed/flustered.

Agendas

Meeting for discussion
parents' evenings

1. Dates
2. Times
3. Reports
4. Display
5. Car Parking

We'll start about
4 pm - finish
when we can.

Senior Management Meeting

Purpose: To consider next term's arrangements for
              parents' evenings
Date: 12th October
Time: 4.00 - 5.00pm
Venue: Library
To attend: Gill R., David C., Bob P., all year
              coordinators. This meeting will be chaired
              by Angela W.

Agenda Items

1 Identifying the purpose
  Co-ordinators are asked to bring feedback from their
  colleagues on the most appropriate use of next term's
  parents evening. We will discuss these and make a
  possible decision on behalf of the staff. This can
  then be taken back for final approval by everyone.

2 Planning to meet the purpose
  We'll discuss what we need to do to meet the purpose
  we have identified. How do we structure the meetings,
  what information do we need to give parents, do we
  need extra displays and so on.

3 Agreeing dates and times
  There are two different sets of dates we need to agree.
  First, we need to suggest dates for the parents'
  evenings and take them back to colleagues. Second, we
  need to suggest a time at which all the staff can
  discuss and work through the issues raised in item 2.

4 Issues for the next meeting
  Please be prepared to raise any items connected with
  parents evenings which need to be discussed at our
  next meeting on the 24th October.

NOTE: Please bring with you diaries, existing report
forms used by colleagues and any other documents helpful
to this meeting.

Agendas are important as they define the purpose of the meeting and set a limit on what's to be covered. The examples above are fictional but do show the difference between an informative agenda and a less than helpful one. Part of the skill in drawing up an agenda is in working to the agreed time span of the meeting. In our experience any after school meeting that goes on for more than about an hour becomes ineffectual. Sometimes it will be impossible for a meeting to finish within such a time span, for example a governors' meeting with twenty agenda items, but if you have control then try to make the meeting **stay on task** and **finish on time**.

Chairperson skills

It is often assumed that chairing skills come naturally – after all, we have so many meetings and so many opportunities to practise. But the reality is different; many chairpersons have had little training and often their poor experiences are simply reinforced every time they chair another meeting. Chairing requires specific skills plus a quick mind and a sense of humour – this checklist will help with some of the practicalities:

Checklist
1　Who is the most suitable person to be chairperson?
It is often better for someone other than the headteacher to chair the meeting. The person with responsibility for the area under discussion is often chosen but they may not be the best if they wish to have a high input.

2　Have minutes, agendas, etc been distributed?
Someone should have clear responsibility for the distribution of minutes, agendas and any other documents or papers needed for the meeting. This is not necessarily the chairperson, but you need to be sure it's being done!

3　Has the room been set up appropriately?
The arrangement and supply of sufficient chairs, refreshments, heating and so on are all important and the chairperson is usually the one who is expected to have seen to this.

---

4 Is the purpose of the meeting clear?
People need to be reminded as to whether the meeting is
consultative, decision making or informational. It helps to set
out the specific aim if there is one.

5 Are you keeping to time and the agenda?
During the meeting it is very important to try and keep to
agenda items and keep an eye on the clock to make sure you
don't run out of time. This is sometimes impossible so it's a
good idea to put missed agenda items on the top of the next
agenda so that they don't get forever ignored.

6 Have you let everyone have their say?
One of the most important chairing skills is to make sure all
those who wish to have the chance to contribute. This means
shutting some people up and encouraging others to participate.

**7 Have you summed up and reflected the decisions and
proposed actions of the meeting?**
It's a good idea to pull together the group consensus or decision
as the meeting goes on and make your own notes to compare
with the minute taker. It's particularly important to have
agreement as to who is going to be responsible for what as a
result of the meeting and to be clear as to any decisions taken.

**8 Have you agreed date, time and venue for any
subsequent meeting?**
It's amazing how easy it is to miss this out in the rush at the
end of a busy meeting, but it makes more work for everyone if
it has to be organised separately.

Minutes

Not many people want to take the minutes at a meeting, yet it is a crucial and highly responsible job. The minute taker needs to be skilled in analysing behaviour, decoding language and setting down clearly decisions, debate and tasks – perhaps that's why so few people want the job! And it's not only the taking of the minutes of a meeting that are vital – their production and distribution is equally important. We once knew a teacher who took excellent minutes and by the end of the day had them distributed to all those who needed them. A PTA secretary also took the minutes of the PTA committee very well but no one received them until the day, or sometimes the hour, before the next meeting started.

What is the purpose of minutes?
Minutes are the formal statement of what was agreed and discussed at a meeting. They serve four main purposes:

* to remind the group what issues were covered at the previous meeting
* to set down responsibilities that have been accepted by group members
* to reflect accurately the feelings and consensus of the meeting
* to record all that happens of significance at the meeting.

The minute taker has a great opportunity to move the meeting on by assisting the chair in gaining summaries of agreements and proposed actions at various points."Now, do you want me to minute the fact that Mike has agreed to represent us at the 'SATs for four-year-olds' conference?" This sort of comment focuses the mind immediately.

What goes in the minutes?
Most importantly minutes should include

* facts (such as the time, date and venue of the meeting)
* names of those present, apologies for absence
* the purpose of the meeting
* decisions taken
* who has agreed to do what
* the main points of agreement and dissension
* date and time of the next meeting.

Minutes cannot cover all that goes on in a meeting; they should be a summary and clearly express the major issues discussed in the

Senior Management Team

Minutes of the meeting of the 12th October

Present: Gill R., Bob P., Angela W. (chair) Jackie M.,
             Derek S., Kay M., Jean G., David C., Clive S.,
             Ruth G.
Apologies: Michael B

Purpose: To consider next term's arrangements for
             parents' evenings.

1   Identifying the purpose

    Year coordinators brought feedback from year-group
    meetings on the most appropriate use of next term's
    meetings. There was considerable agreement amongst year
    groups, although there was discussion about the
    suggestion from the Year 6 group that parents should be
    given hard information about their child's performance
    relative to other children in the year.

    There was sympathy for this view but it was felt that we
    weren't experienced enough with the SATs this year to
    begin this. It was important, though, and would be
    brought up again next year.

    The meeting agreed that the purpose of next term's
    parents' evening would be to let parents see all of
    their children's work but to concentrate our comments
    for this year on English, Maths and Science.

    This to go back to year groups for final approval.

2   Planning to meet the purpose

    There was much more discussion here, as might have been
    expected. The main points of discussion were
    • Would parents want to discuss curr. areas other than
       the core subjects?
    • Will there still be time to discuss non-curriculum
       issues?
    • How can we let them know what we are doing?
    • How can we make sure parents are getting the same deal
       from all of us?
    • Will this take more time than we have got?
    • Will our display concentrate on the three core areas
       or on all of the curriculum, as in the past?

    Following discussion it was agreed that

meeting. It might be a good idea to let different members of the group take turns at minuting the meeting so they can all experience the frustrations and difficulties of recording the events of a poorly run meeting, and hopefully, the satisfaction of minuting an effective one.

Conclusion

Badly run meetings can cause	Well run meetings can
• low morale	• move the development process forward
• poor motivation	• make decisions
• dissent and back-biting	• allocate tasks
• lack of decision making	• keep a check on progress
• poor accountability	• dispel rumour and suspicion
• ineffective curriculum development	• build teams
• frustration and dissatisfaction.	• generate a sense of achievement.

One of the clearest messages of this book is that development planning is about more than simply creating a plan and more than achieving the targets contained within that plan. It's really about managing and being part of an effective school. Contained within successful development planning are issues concerned with motivation, climate, the community, organisation, job descriptions, joint involvement and more.

Because the whole process is concerned with so much of the life of a school it seems inevitable that close links will – or should – be established between each school's development plan and the growing procedure of school reviews.

The growth of accountability

Schools are now more accountable than they have been in the past. A decrease in public confidence, an increase in political interest and a growing understanding of what democratic involvement in education might mean for schools have created a situation in which schools are more conscious of the need to respond to the public and, in particular, to their governing bodies.

But accountability has also grown in another form. Local authorities have, to some extent, been marginalised by many of the recent changes in education. Some see this as deliberate, others as just the consequence of the changed nature of the world we live in. At one extreme, schools do have more responsibility than they did before, even if they are still trying to work out whether they have any more power. At the other extreme – and despite protestations to the contrary – central government has taken a firmer grip on the activities of schools than it held in the past.

This has left the LEAs with less responsibilities for schools – but those responsibilities are no less crucial than before. One of the most important – and potentially one of the most influential – is the responsibility to review the provision of education in the schools in its area.

In other words, the LEA has been given the responsibility of monitoring the effectiveness of schools on behalf of the public and the government. Such outside monitoring, while seen as a threat by some, cannot be altogether unreasonable. (In the same way that many people express support for an independent police complaints procedure on the grounds that it is difficult to be prosecutor and judge at the same time, so it is difficult to argue against some form of external monitoring in education.)

The growth of formal reviews

To a degree, LEAs have always discharged this responsibility, although the way in which it was carried out varied greatly from authority to authority. For a long time the use of either the term 'Adviser' or 'Inspector' denoted an authority's approach to the way it reviewed its schools, but even within those broad definitions there were considerable differences.

In some authorities, schools were asked to do very little and hardly noticed the authority carrying out any reviewing at all. In others, the headteacher might receive a visit from an adviser or inspector to talk over a number of issues. Occasionally that inspector might visit certain classrooms. Often a school was expected to undertake its own review, to be accountable for itself. It was this view which lay behind the creation of some of the checklists we discuss elsewhere.

Formal reviews were only usually carried out when a lack of public confidence in a school became manifest or when an inspectorial visit produced evidence of something seriously wrong.

In the last few years, this has begun to change. More and more authorities are accepting that their new responsibility involves the formal review of schools on a regular basis. Inspectors and advisers are finding that their new role consists of a pattern of visits to schools, often in teams of two or three, interspersed with explanatory meetings with the governors, headteacher, teachers and parents. Increasingly, the results of those reviews are available to the public.

The implications of formal reviews

There are a number of implications in the move to formal reviews which should concern schools.

1   The definition of what represents effective schooling
If schools are to be reviewed, if the results of those reviews are to be made public and if the inevitable comparisons between schools are going to be made on the basis of those reviews, then it is only reasonable to expect someone to define the criteria for reasonable

success. We spoke earlier in the book about the importance job descriptions have in letting people judge the level of success in their job. In the same way, schools which are being reviewed have a right to know the criteria around which judgements are being made.

Unfortunately, there is experience across the country of authorities not declaring the criteria they are using or, in some cases, quite clearly not having any such criteria. In practice, many review teams have been forced into creating their own criteria which may, of course, be different from those of other review teams in the same authority. They will almost certainly be different from review teams in other authorities. The outcome is that comparisons between schools become meaningless and the accountability procedure weakened.

2 The breadth of a formal review
Even when review teams have some idea of what represents effective schooling, the usefulness of a review is affected by the breadth across which it operates. If a team spends two or three days in a school looking at every aspect of the school's organisation and delivery the chances are that some parts of that review will be superficial; the chances are, too, that some aspects of the school will always be found wanting. This further diminishes the usefulness of the review procedure.

3 The experience of the review team
At the moment, there aren't enough inspectors and advisers employed by most authorities to provide the experience necessary to review the separate phases of the education service. However willing and determined they may be, there is likely to be something flawed about a system in which someone with twenty-five years of infant school experience is reviewing the teaching of classics, or someone with twenty years experience of running a secondary science department is reviewing an infant school.

4 The contribution of the school
At a time when so much of what we are learning about educational management is stressing the need for appropriate collaborative work between all those involved in creating effective education for children, many reviews are recreating the top-down model with a vengeance. Yet a review team is with a school for only a limited period; each school must have valuable experiences and insights which can contribute towards their own reviews.

Solving these problems is not going to be easy but we believe that school development plans can make a real contribution.

Solving the problems

If the previous section seemed like a criticism of the whole formal review procedure it wasn't meant to be; we were simply trying to identify some of the problems. Formal reviews have a number of important advantages. They

- provide a mechanism through which schools can be accountable
- provide a means of gathering evidence about the nature of schooling over a wide geographical area
- can provide evidence which can be used to support arguments about funding for resources of various kinds
- can provide each school with a cooler, more reflective view of what is happening.

For all these reasons we think the formal review of schools is a good idea. What needs to be done is to maximise the potential they offer. We think the linking of reviews to development plans is an important part of this process for a number of reasons.

1 It can provide a focus for the review
A review linked to a school development plan should be more focused than one which isn't linked to anything. The plan provides evidence to the reviewers of what the school thinks are its important targets and where it is in the attainment of those targets.

This provides the review team with two important functions. First, to look for evidence to see whether the school is right in its own evaluation of what has and has not been achieved. Second, to look at the range of priorities and targets identified to see whether the school is failing to respond to areas of obvious importance.

Given the limited time over which reviews have to take place, a focused review is always going to be more effective than an unfocused one.

2 It can allow the school to retain a sense of ownership
Without a sense of ownership, the ability of individuals and their organisations to respond positively to anything is much reduced. A school which is reviewed against a set of criteria which are imposed from outside is less likely to respond positively to the results of that review, however well intentioned and accurate they may be. A review which takes place against a set of criteria which are largely of the school's making is likely to receive greater attention from all those concerned with it.

3 It allows schools to be reviewed on what they have done

There seems little point in recommending and encouraging schools to take part in the process of development planning – of defining priorities, creating targets, causing action and evaluating that action – and then reviewing them on something completely different. If a review is to be purposeful it needs to address itself first to what has been done rather than what hasn't been done.

This isn't to say that what hasn't been done in a school shouldn't feature as part of the review – more about that later. What it does mean is that the balance of the review is changed in favour of looking at that which has happened rather than that which has not.

4 It can create a climate of achievement rather than one of failure

The reality is that many people working in schools at the moment are more demoralised than they have been for some time. Many are also concerned about the review procedure – you have only to observe the frantic activity and worry which precedes many reviews to realise that.

Focusing the review on the achievements of the school's development plan will make a contribution towards altering the climate within schools to one which is more positive. Because of the importance of the reviews to schools, and because so many public judgements will inevitably be formed as a result of them, their influence is going to be considerable.

If we believe that it is ultimately more productive within school to catch people doing things 'approximately right' (see Section 3.13) then it must also be so for review teams. In looking closely at the targets a school has set itself – and the appropriateness of those targets – reviews have the opportunity of influencing the climate of schools for some years to come.

5 It maintains the benefits of an outsider's 'cool eye'

It is important that schools should be reviewed from a more neutral stance than self-evaluation can allow. Choosing the development plan as the focus for that doesn't alter this at all – if anything it is likely to increase the effectiveness of the review; the 'cool eye' will be cast over something that matters to everyone.

There is a danger that we may be charged with suggesting that reviews should always be supportive of schools; that they should act as a cover-up for some of the inadequacies rather than as an accountability procedure. Nothing could be more wrong.

We expect some schools to be criticised heavily as a result of the reviews which take place. What concerns us is the focus of that criticism, its fairness to the school and its usefulness to those for whom the review is undertaken.

To send a review team into a school and ask it to find things to criticise is probably the easiest job in education. Teaching, the planning of learning, the motivation, discipline and support of young people and the organisation of schools is such a complex and difficult task that it can almost never be got 'right'.

A review along these lines is simply unproductive. But a review which looks at the appropriateness of a school's chosen priorities, which helps it to judge the success with which it has achieved its self-identified targets, which looks closely at the management of these successes and failures and which contributes a well-formed external perspective, is a review which is wholly useful.

We think that development plans and reviews are, rightly, a part of the same process.

The Role of the Headteacher 5.7

The nature of any role changes constantly as situations change. The change is usually gradual, but is sometimes more rapid because of some exceptional internal or external impetus.

In recent years the role of headteacher has been changing comparatively rapidly. This has been due to a variety of interrelated influences. These influences have included

- the increased attention paid to education since James Callaghan's 1976 'Ruskin College Speech'
- the tendency for education to be blamed for the country's poor economic performance
- the growth of political philosophies which are antagonistic to the power of local authorities and which emphasise the market economy
- the development of notions of accountability
- the application of management theories to schools.

The rate of change has increased drastically because of a spate of education and other legislation, culminating in the 1988 Education Reform Act.

In a paper entitled 'Education Managers – Paradigms Lost', Professor H O Jenkins of the Polytechnic of Wales writes:

> "Heads are faced with mounting pressures in managing their schools effectively as government demands on education grow daily. The introduction of local management of schools with devolved financial powers and a new role for the governing body; the possibility of opting out; the bringing in of a national curriculum, pupil testing and new examinations; parental choice of schools; the creation of close links between school and industry; performance evaluation and teacher appraisal; all are manifest indicators of a formidable array of managerial tasks facing the head. Less obvious, however, but equally powerful, are the demands to raise standards in schools and to create in them, with the help of the Training Commission, a spirit of enterprise. All these demands, against the usual background of uncertainty about levels of finance, a growing shortage of teachers in key areas of the curriculum and low teacher morale, do appear overwhelming."

Planning for school development provides a way of coping with the "overwhelming" demands described by Professor Jenkins. At the same time, the nature of headship puts the responsibility for initiating and overseeing such planning firmly in the court of the headteacher.

The Articles of Government for County Schools state unequivocally that:

> *"...the headteacher is responsible for the internal organisation and management of the school and for exercising supervision over the teaching and non-teaching staff..."*

Implementation of a school development plan is a means of enabling a headteacher to fulfil his or her responsibilities for organisation and management and for supervision of staff.

A headteacher is many things:

- An establisher of systems. A school needs to have established systems so that as things arise they can be dealt with. There needs to be a defined management structure, a job description for each member of staff (teaching and non-teaching), and a fairly detailed staff handbook. There needs to be a comprehensive filing system, and a book-keeping system.
- A setter of minimum requirements. Such requirements cover children's work and behaviour, staff duties, curriculum development, approaches to teaching and classroom organisation.
- A communicator. To children, staff, parents, community, governors, LEA, etc.
- A curriculum leader. Having a view of the school's overall curriculum, and guiding teachers through their curriculum responsibilities and their class teaching, contributing to and developing that curriculum.
- A planner articulating the vision of the future and setting the course towards its fulfilment – including individual responsibilities and time scales
- A delegator. Assigning tasks and areas of responsibilities – allowing people the resources to meet them. Providing encouragement and monitoring progress.
- A financial manager. Allocating resources according to needs. Monitoring expenditure. Reporting to governors and seeking approval as necessary.
- A marketer. Presenting the school to its public. Building its image. Drawing the school into positive attention. Attracting the parents of potential pupils.

- An arbiter of behaviour. Establishing, communicating, maintaining and enforcing standards of children's behaviour.
- A recruiter of staff. Identifying vacancies, advertising, appointing.
- A booster of morale. Reassuring and encouraging staff when the pressures grow.
- A team leader. Co-ordinating activities. Setting an example of enthusiasm, involvement, and professional competence.
- An agent of the governing body. Acting on the governors' behalf according to their policies, providing them with information and recommendations, keeping in regular contact with them and especially with the chairperson.
- A developer of staff. Seeing individual staff regularly to discuss progress, development and training needs – agreeing on future action.
- A consultant. Consulting widely, particularly with staff and also with others, so that decisions are based on a broad base of information and knowledge of other people's perceptions.
- A pastor. Being available to children, staff, parents and others to listen and provide counsel.
- An instigator, overseer and enabler. From a unique position it is often possible to see things that need to be done. It is then the headteacher's responsibility to see that they are done.
- A quality controller. Monitoring the performance of staff and of children.

Introducing, devising, implementing and monitoring a school development plan is, essentially, the responsibility of the headteacher. However, a headteacher cannot – and should not – do any of this alone. A headteacher who says, "Here is the plan, now get on with it", is likely to face problems. As John Adair says:

> "There is a common sense principle that the more a group (or individual) shares in the thinking and decision making process the more it is likely to be committed to making the agreed plan work. But keep a firm control of the process."

Headteachers need to have vision. They need to have an image of the sort of school they would like to see. They need to share their vision with others, but they must also share other people's visions, recognising that they do not have a monopoly on idealism. What is important is not that everyone works towards the fulfilment of the headteacher's dream but that there is some sort of corporate vision of the future.

An essential aspect of a headteacher's role is to help establish an ethos in which joint planning is possible and in which realistic targets can be achieved. In such an ethos staff can feel able to contribute to formulating a plan and feel that commitment to a plan is not something which can be achieved overnight. Nor is it something that can be created just for the production of a school development plan and ignored for anything else. School development planning requires a situation in which people feel valued for the contribution they can make. Creation of such an ethos is something which takes an enormous degree of skill and sensitivity.

> "The effective executive makes strength productive. He knows that one cannot build on weakness. To achieve results, one has to use all the available strengths – the strengths of associates, the strengths of the superior, and one's own strengths. These strengths are the true opportunities. To make strength productive is the unique purpose of organisation. It cannot, of course, overcome the weaknesses with which each one of us is abundantly endowed. But it can make them irrelevant. Its task is to use the strength of each man as a building block for joint performance."
>
> Peter Drucker, *The Effective Executive*

In most cases it will be the headteacher who establishes the procedures for drawing up a school development plan. He or she will also implement those procedures and probably physically produce the actual plan. The original GRIDS project envisaged a co-ordinator "designated to be responsible for planning and organising the whole exercise". It is interesting that during the pilot phase:

> "In four of the five LEAs the heads designated themselves as school co-ordinators and in the one LEA where scale post teachers were originally selected as co-ordinators the heads had all assumed this role by the end of the year."
>
> *GRIDS Primary School Handbook*

It is, however, essential that the headteacher consults widely and involves others fully at all stages of the process.

Once the school development plan has been prepared, it is the headteacher's responsibility to communicate that plan to those who have an interest in it. It may be that not everyone will want or need the full version of the plan and that for some audiences a shorter, summary plan will be sufficient. Certainly teachers will need a copy of the full plan. Most members of the non-teaching staff might only require a shortened version. This shortened version will probably be enough for governors and the local education authority, although the full plan should be available on request for both of these. It is also worth remembering that, on presentation to the governing body, the school development plan becomes a public document and as such is accessible to parents and others.

Finally, it is the headteacher's responsibility to monitor the implementation of the plan. As with most things, part of this task can be delegated, but the responsibility remains with the head to ensure that monitoring takes place. This monitoring is not something that can be left until the end of the period covered by the plan, but is a continuous process. The actual form of the monitoring will depend on the nature of the activity but a variety of strategies can be used. These include regular meetings with individual members of staff, with groups and with the whole staff; observations in classrooms and elsewhere; collection of children's books, teachers records, etc; the careful use of 'performance indicators' or 'success criteria' and 'market research' surveys.

Headteachers must be clear about what is monitored and what criteria they are using. Whenever possible, other people should also be aware of these things.

6 Case Studies

The following four accounts describe some attempts to introduce school development plans into individual schools.

6.1   Pondside

6.2   Taunton Grange

6.3   Sunningvale Wood

6.4   Dawson Road

Pondside 6.1

Pondside Junior School is situated on the rural fringe of an Outer London borough in an area which, although now absorbed into suburban sprawl, still retains a great deal of its village identity. It is a large school with around 380 children on roll. The vast majority are from middle class families.

Angela Dickens was appointed to the headship of Pondside in January 1988. She is in her second headship, having previously worked for a different authority. She replaced a long-standing headteacher who was known and respected throughout the area. The deputy headteacher has been at the school for several years and had spent a period as acting head.

The school has always enjoyed a very good reputation in the local community. Yet the new headteacher recognised that there were things that needed to change.

Mrs Dickens believes that the style of developmental planning has to reflect the situation of the school and also that it is very dependent upon relationships within the school. "We are in the process of building up relationships," she says. "I would have used a very different approach if I had been here for ten years." She also says that there was no way she could have produced a planning document – however informal or superficial – at her previous school. "The relationships were insufficient. We weren't ready to see the school moving as a whole – teachers were still entirely involved in their own classroom situation."

Mike Alexander, the deputy headteacher, explains that the thing that really swung the situation at Pondside was the production of short term objectives. "These were achievable and people could see the results. Things were visibly being done and they provided the impetus to get to the long term." This point is supported by one of the teachers who says, "It's good to know where you are going. People sometimes jump on to bandwagons and never follow things through. Knowing where you are going next is vital." Another teacher – appointed to the school after the first plan had already been produced – adds, "It gives everyone a common goal. It pulls people together. In my last school we were working independently and in isolation – but not here."

The head, deputy and staff lay great emphasis on the consultation process. "It gives people the opportunity to express their ideas," says Angela Dickens. "They can look at the development plan and say, 'I feel part of it'." According to Mike Alexander, the atmosphere of consultation makes it very easy to go to people and ask them to think about something.

Involvement in preparing a development plan reinforced and heightened the headteacher's belief in the importance of communication.

"Until you go through this sort of exercise you don't really appreciate the importance of communication," she says now. "No matter what lip-service you have paid to it before, now it becomes a crucial activity."

"With the existence of a plan there is improved two-way communication – because people were consulted in the first place. Now staff meetings really mean something. The development plan has cleared the way for other things and we're not just dealing with the superficial. Action can be taken more quickly. Problems are dealt with quickly instead of being allowed to build up."

Mr Alexander says that there is a feeling within the school that "things are going on". "There is no panic to get things done, though. Things are planned far ahead of time, rather than dealt with through crisis management."

The headteacher and deputy have found value in their membership of a school development 'network group'. Once a term they meet with the heads and deputies of two other schools – one of them new to the idea of school development plans, and one of them having been involved for some time. The meetings have no formal agenda but give people a chance to share notes and exchange ideas. "It gives us extra strength," says Mike Alexander. "No one tries to take over, and no one feels threatened."

They also gain support from INSET provided by the authority and from consultations with a primary inspector and an external consultant funded by the education department.

The headteacher does not feel daunted by external initiatives overriding what is in the plan. "The National Curriculum, LMS and so on can be merged into the plan," she says, "and not throw it off course." For her deputy, the school development plan "gives confidence to cope with things as they arise."

Now that developmental planning is established at Pondside, Angela Dickens recognises that things would not have worked if she had said to the staff: "Here is the plan. Let's get on with it."

"You have to appreciate that there are people who can do some things better than you can do them yourself. You have to respect the fact that people have strengths. You have to make everybody feel wanted." She has also found that the direction in which the plan is leading the school is supported not only by the staff but also by the local inspectorate, HMI, and the school's governing body. For the future she sees that the whole procedure could lead nicely into some form of constructive staff appraisal.

Mike Alexander now feels that the development plan, having been dependent on the existing situation within the school, has done a great deal to help create an ethos. "It has helped to bring everybody together. In a way it has more side effects than direct effects," he says. "What is actually written down is almost incidental. Development is far more than some sheets of paper – it's a process."

Taunton Grange

Taunton Grange Primary School is an inner city school set in a neighbourhood of some deprivation and classed as being in a Social Priority Area. There are 290 children on roll covering the full primary age-range, with a further twelve children in a special needs unit. Nick Morris has been headteacher at the school for nine years.

Nick Morris explains that for five or six years the school has operated what he loosely calls a staff appraisal scheme and that this had been linked with planning for INSET. "I talked to each teacher about their classroom practice, their professional development and any post of responsibility. The emphasis was very much on classroom development. These discussions always led to the setting of individual targets which served as the basis for any courses."

Nick Morris says that the discussions helped him to identify the needs of the school. "The big flaw was in the time element. Time was against us in every aspect. There was never enough time for talking, and we were always setting targets which were unrealistic in the time available."

When the school became involved in a school development project promoted by the LEA, the headteacher was able to build on what had gone before. "What I wanted to do was not to scrap what we had but to develop it and align it with what was being suggested."

At the beginning of the summer term, all teachers were given a questionnaire. This asked them to think about what the school needed to do in a whole range of specified areas. "Teachers had the opportunity to express their opinion of their own development and of school development before we actually sat down to talk," says Mr Morris.

Individual discussions took place towards the end of the summer term. They were based on the questionnaires as a starting point, with the teachers' viewpoints being compared and matched with the headteacher's.

"After that, we all got together and talked in general terms about school development. We talked about what we had done as a school over the previous year. We talked about whether we had achieved our individual targets and about what had prevented us if we hadn't." Nick Morris observes that the most difficult part was getting people to speak on an informal basis in this open forum.

During the summer holiday Nick Morris collated all the notes from the questionnaires, the individual discussions and the open forum. He used these notes to produce draft documents stating individual targets for classroom practice and for areas of responsibility. From these he was able to state the targets for the school as a whole. He says that this "gave people individual targets within the overall team performance. If you take the old cliché that we're all here for the good of the children, then we can only achieve that by looking to develop ourselves."

The drafts were given out on the day before the autumn term. The target sheets for classroom practice went only to the individuals concerned. Everything else was given to everybody. Teachers were given time to read the documents and to see if they were a true representation of discussions. "Then we all got together to decide how, practically, we were going to set about achieving the targets. We also talked about how in-service training could be used to help us to fulfil the targets." There is something of a problem in that INSET has to be planned for the financial year while the development plan covers the school year. This is only partly overcome by having a rolling plan of two years, but Nick Morris wonders if they ought to re-time the development plan to coincide with INSET.

Another problem he anticipates concerns changeover of staff. "It's OK if we appoint specifically to replace someone who is leaving, but not so easy with falling numbers and changed incentive allowances." Recent recruitment difficulties – leading to lowered expectations of what a teacher can be asked to do – are also causing some rethinking.

Yet Mr Morris remains convinced of the value of planned development. "I'm amazed and delighted that those teachers who are established on the staff have dealt with the situation and kept it going," he says. "They have coped with staff changes and are determined that the plan will succeed – wanting to see the end result."

Despite all his efforts, Morris still has to convert the governing body. "I feel that I've not yet convinced governors that it is something worth doing. They still tend to say 'You're the professional; we've got every faith in you; just keep us informed.' That's fine when everything is going well, but what happens if something goes wrong?"

He feels, however, that the school has devised something which is a valuable tool. "What we have is a simplified system of staff appraisal intertwined within what we call a school development plan." He is quick to stress that the plan is not a cut and dried document but one that has many flexibilities. "We have to take into account changes in personnel. We have to respond to issues as they arise from outside. And we have to bear in mind changing expectations on the part of the community."

Nor is the procedure for drawing up the plan a fixed one. "The important thing is that we have started. But just because we did it this way once, doesn't mean that it's the only way. As with everything, we have to devise procedures that suit our own situation."

As for the teaching staff: "They see the instigation of a development plan as something which is purposeful and as something in which they can be involved. They feel in touch with it and they feel that they have a valuable part to play in the development of the school rather than being told what to do."

Sunningvale Wood Infant School is set in a fairly affluent area of a small market town. Sylvia Ward was appointed headteacher in January 1988, having previously been deputy head of a large primary school.

When Miss Ward was appointed she felt that everyone was telling her to have a school development plan – colleagues, inspectors, induction course tutors. She took their advice and set about the process, even though nobody had been very clear about what a development plan actually was. She is now the first to admit that she made some mistakes along the way.

"When I arrived at the school," she says, "the first thing I had to do was talk to all staff. I asked each teacher the same question – If you had got my job, what would be the first thing you would want to do?" There were some things that everybody agreed on, such as replacing the reading scheme. Some of the suggestions were much more mundane, like the suggestion of knocking down a wall to get easier access to the toilets.

From the ideas put forward by the staff, Sylvia Ward drew up a development plan. But here, she says, she made her first big mistake. "I assumed that everyone actually wanted things to change," she says. "But really there was no undercurrent for a development plan of any sort."

"My second mistake was to make the plan unmanageable. There were too many things planned for too short a period of time. Each item in the plan was accompanied by a detailed and complex list of 'steps to implementation' which really served to make the whole plan even more inaccessible." She now realises that people felt threatened. She had – by her own decision – made plans for change when there was no climate for change. The result was cynicism. "People were asking, 'Who the heck is this dreadful woman who has been foisted upon us?'"

Despite the mistakes and failures, however, Miss Ward remained convinced that developmental planning was the right way forward. She and the deputy head decided to enrol in the authority's pilot scheme for school development. They realised that the staff as a whole needed to be convinced and to be involved. One way they saw of doing this was to take the two people most cynical about school development along to the INSET sessions. One of them became a convert who then helped to influence other people. The other left the school a short time later.

"There were still a lot of people who were not feeling involved and I wanted to find a way of including everybody," Sylvia Ward observes. "I prepared a questionnaire. It had forty-two questions with a separate page for each question." She soon realised that it was much too long and the most telling moment was when she heard a teacher say, "I thought self-evaluation was about more selective work, not more work."

"I knew that now was a time for retrenchment," she says. "Self-evaluation, development plan and questionnaire all became no-no words. We dropped all explicit reference to the subject although it was still there implicitly."

In time the headteacher became aware that slowly the climate was changing and that common understandings were growing. "We were beginning to pull together in the sense that we were all sharing similar aims. People were also becoming aware of external pressures, such as the National Curriculum and a forthcoming routine inspection. They could see that things needed to be done but knew that we couldn't do everything at once. They began to see how a development plan would help. We would then be able to say to inspectors or anyone else, 'Here is our plan. This is what we have done and this is what we are going to do.'"

Now the whole process has started again. This time it has teachers' understanding, involvement and support. It is also a simpler process than before, starting with a brief survey and leading to an outline plan which can be enlarged when the time is ready.

Learning from her own mistakes, Sylvia Ward is able to advise colleagues how to avoid some of the major pitfalls. "Take account of the existing climate. Beware of making false assumptions. Make the plan realistic. Make the plan everyone's. If possible, don't formulate the plan until everyone knows what's going to be in it."

She is also able to take heart from the comments of an HMI who toured the school as part of a National Curriculum survey. Afterwards he told her, "You may not have a plan on paper, but it does exist in everyone's head – and you're all talking about the same things!"

Dawson Road Primary School serves an area which includes a large council estate as well as fairly expensive private housing. The school was formed as a result of amalgamation of separate infant and junior schools in 1985. The amalgamation, which took place at a time of industrial action, had been opposed by governors, parents and teachers and led to a period of unsettlement. The current headteacher is David Peters who had been head of the junior school since 1981.

During the spring term 1987 Mr Peters was granted a secondment to research into primary school management. Following this time the staff held a day conference on a Saturday in a local hotel. "I wanted teachers to share something of what I had done and what I had learned," David Peters explains. "We invited speakers from industry and commerce, and as a result of their input, the staff as a whole decided that we ought to plan for the future rather than be continually reacting to things as they occurred." At the end of the day David Peters was given the task of surveying opinion and collating results.

"I didn't like the published schemes with lots of questions and check lists," he says. "They seemed much too complicated and I could see a danger of bits of paper becoming more important than the end result." Instead, he devised a three-question questionnaire. Teachers were each asked about what had been achieved in their specialist areas over the past year, what needed to be done in the coming year, and what they thought should be the school's overall priorities for the future.

From this simple format – and having talked to each teacher individually – the headteacher collated, under various headings, a list of 125 suggestions of things that needed to be done. "Some of the ideas were straightforward and could be dealt with in a matter of minutes. Others were much more far-reaching. It was clear that it would be impossible to do everything in one year." Each teacher was given a copy of the list and was asked to mark each suggestion with a number between one and four where number one meant high priority and number four meant not a priority at all.

"The results of this were very interesting," David Peters says. "There were some things that everybody agreed about and others that received the full range of one to four. There were also some very striking contradictions among what was being put forward." He decided that using the numbers as a crude voting system would lead to distorted results and chose instead to employ his 'professional judgement'. "Using the evidence gathered through consultation, I was able to identify needs and indicate ways in which those needs would be met. All this was listed under appropriate headings with some items earmarked for the coming year and others, in less detail, for the two years after that."

The school now had a draft development plan which the headteacher was able to present to the staff for their approval. "Later I presented it to the governing body but I don't really think they took much notice of it. The second time around I presented them with the plan saying that this was the staff's plan and asking them to adopt it as their own. This made them consider it much more carefully and give it some degree of commitment," he says. Now when the Chairman of Governors visits the school he asks the headteacher to go through the development plan and report on progress. For subsequent development plans Mr Peters has asked governors to get involved at a much earlier stage – before the plan is actually drafted. He has also tried to involve non-teaching staff but with limited success.

Much of the development plan is deliberately set out in fairly broad terms. At least once a term the headteacher meets with individual teachers and talks with them about their tasks. It is in these discussions that more detailed targets are set and a tighter time scale established.

Dawson Road's development plan covers all aspects of school life. "I think it's important that the plan has something for everybody," says David Peters. "I also think that we need to show that we are aware of the school as a totality. If an inspector or someone tells us that we need to do something about drama, for example, then we can say: yes, we know and that is why we've marked it down for attention at some time in the future – but in the meantime we think that something else is more pressing."

The headteacher feels that the development plan puts the teaching staff in a strong position. As one of the teachers points out, "We know what is expected of of us. Things aren't sprung upon us without warning." He also feels that the planning process strengthens his own position. "I feel I am in control of the situation," he says, "and can demonstrate that the school knows where it is going."

There does have to be a certain amount of flexibility, though. "During the first year something arose that we would have been foolish to ignore just because it wasn't down on our plan for immediate action. We had to revise the plan." More recently some unanticipated staffing changes and a long-term absence have meant other changes. "In that situation you have to decide what is essential and what can be put off until later," David Peters observes.

After two years the headteacher is aware of the dangers of the planning process becoming too rigid. For year two the school went through almost exactly the same procedures to devise a plan, but then the approach, and the format, was varied. "For one thing we didn't need to generate another 125 suggestions each year!" Mr Peters says. "We have got enough ideas outstanding and other things have emerged from various discussions. On top of all that, the National Curriculum and LMS have given us a few things to consider – and so has a detailed inspection report." There will still be plenty of discussion and consultation, though, and the whole thing is still kept quite simple.

"The plan itself is only a means to an end," David Peters says. "The important bit is the development not the development plan. And the test of that is in the effect that it has on children's learning."

Concluding Remarks

Our editor put us under no little pressure to call this section 'Conclusion' but we can't; it sounds too neat. Development planning is already under threat of being seen as more rational than it is without us adding to it by suggesting that we can form conclusions!

Development planning cannot, by itself, create an effective school in which children and young people receive a focused and appropriate education which helps them to develop intellectually, spiritually, physically and emotionally. It is becoming increasingly clear that while the planning process can often make a considerable contribution to the overall organisation of a school, it also feeds off that organisation.

What it can do is to help clear a path through what appears at times to be an increasingly impenetrable jungle of conflicting demands, requirements and pressures. In revealing priorities and contributing towards a clearer sense of purpose, development planning can help us to focus on what really matters for our own school. It can help us to develop appropriate strategies for achieving those priorities and can help to provide an education more appropriate than ever to the young people we teach.

There is a necessary and strong element of rationality in all this and careful, analytical thought is vital if effective development plans are to be produced. Nevertheless, having built the ship with as much care as possible, we launch it into increasingly choppy seas where the unexpected and irrational have a habit of ruining the best of our plans.

This doesn't mean to say that development planning is a waste of time. It does mean that we will only maximise the possibilities if we can combine the careful construction of the plan with a constant vigilance in its management. We don't necessarily need to make wholesale changes to our plan all the time. Indeed, if we do then there seems little point in having a plan at all. But we do need to be aware of when to make the subtle alterations, the small moves and the careful re-alignments. It is those which will keep our plan afloat.

Development planning is not a new idea. Many years ago, Seneca pointed out that "Without a sense of direction, no wind is favourable to a sailor" and, presumably, he was only repeating remarks made on the beaches and in the cafés for hundreds, perhaps thousands, of years before him.

Yet in the weekend before these concluding remarks were being written, we worked with a group of headteachers representing about thirty different schools in widely differing locations. Out of that group only one school had a clearly defined development plan and only four more were in the process of creating one.

There is still a long way to go. Although progress to the implementation of an effective development plan can sometimes be slow, the good news is that we have seen schools revitalised and transformed by a careful and committed approach to development planning. Our hope is that this book will be of some practical help to headteachers and teachers along the way.

Bibliography

R Abbot, S Steadman and M Birchenough, *Grids: Primary School Handbook*, 2nd edition (Longman, London, 1988)

J Adair, *Effective Leadership* (Pan, London, 1983)

S Ball, *The Micro-Politics of the School* (Methuen, London, 1987)

K Blanchard and R Lorber, *Putting the One Minute Manager to Work* (Fontana, London, 1984)

Bromley, the London Borough, *Developing Your School – Making School Development Plans Work* (Bromley/ Fieldwork Ltd, 1989)

R Carter, J Martin, B Mayblin and M Munday, *Systems, Management and Change* (Open University Press/Harper and Row, Milton Keynes, 1984)

A Coulson, *The Managerial Work of Primary Headteachers* (Sheffield City Polytechnic, 1986)

I Craig (ed), *Primary Management in the 1990s* (Longman, London, 1989)

I Craig, *Primary School Management in Action*, 2nd edition (Longman, London, 1989)

C Day, P Whitaker and D Wren, *Appraisal and Professional Development in Primary Schools* (Open University Press, Milton Keynes 1987)

W Dyer, *Team Building – Issues and Alternatives* (Addison Wesley, 1987)

E Eisner, *The Art of Educational Evaluation* (Falmer Press, Lewes, 1985)

M Fullan, *The Meaning of Educational Change* (Teachers' College Press, New York, 1982)

C H Godefroy and J Clark, *The Complete Time Management System* (Piatkus, 1989)

H L Gray (ed), *Management Consultancy in Schools* (Cassell, London, 1988)

D Hamilton, D Jenkins, C King, B MacDonald and M Parlett (eds), *Beyond the Numbers Game* (MacMillan, Basingstoke, 1978)

C Handy and R Aitken, *Understanding Schools as Organisations* (Penguin, London, 1986)

D Hargreaves, *Interpersonal Relations and Education* (RKP, London, 1978)

D Hargreaves, D Hopkins, M Leask, J Connoly and P Robinson, *Planning for School Development – Advice to Governors, Headteachers and Teachers* (DES, 1989)

D Hargreaves, D Hopkins and M Leask, *The Management of Development Planning – A Paper for Local Education Authorities* (DES, 1990)

P J Holly and G Southworth, *The Developing Primary School* (Falmer Press, Lewes, 1989)

ILEA, *Keeping the School Under Review: the Primary School* (ILEA, London, 1982)

ILEA, *Improving Primary Schools – Report of the Thomas Committee* (ILEA, London, 1985)

H O Jenkins, 'Education Managers – Paradigms Lost' in *Studies in Educational Adminisitration*, 51, 1989

A Leigh, *Twenty Ways to Manage Better* (Institute of Personnel Management, London, 1984)

R Lessem, *Developmental Management, Principles of Holistic Business* (Blackwell, Oxford, 1990)

G Morgan, *Images of Organisation* (Sage Publications, Beverley Hills, 1986)

P Mortimore, P Sammons, L Stoll, D Lewis and R Ecob, *School Matters: The Junior Years* (Open Books, Wells, 1988)

T Peters and N Austin, *A Passion for Excellence: The Leadership Difference* (Fontana Books, New York and London, 1985)

D Playfoot, M Skelton and G Southworth, *The Primary School Management Book* (Mary Glasgow Publications, London, 1989)

A Pollard and S Tann, *Reflective Teaching in the Primary School: A Handbook for the Classroom* (Cassell, London, 1988)

I Rodger and J Richardson, *Self-Evaluation for Primary Schools* (Hodder and Stoughton, Sevenoaks, 1985)

Salford Education Department, *Profile '82* (City of Salford Education Department, 1982)

M Skelton, 'School Development Plans', in *Primary File Series 2* (Mary Glasgow Publications, London 1989)

G Southworth, *Readings in Primary School Management* (Falmer Press, London, 1987)

L Stenhouse, *An Introduction to Curriculum Research and Development* (Heinemann, London, 1975)

D Styan *et al*, *Developing School Management – The Way Foreward, A Report by the School Management Task Force* (HMSO, London, 1990)

Surrey, School Development Plans – Local Management of Surrey Schools (Surrey County Council, 1990)

N Thomas, 'A Tool for Improvement', *Times Educational Supplement*, 6.3.87

D Trethowan, *Target Setting* (The Industrial Society, London, 1983)

P Whittaker, *The Primary Head* (Heinemann, London, 1983)

Wiltshire, *Working Together – Planning School Development* (Wiltshire, 1990)